HOLIDAYS AT HOME

HOLIDAYS AT HOME

Crafts to Celebrate the Season

EDITED BY DAWN ANDERSON

Martingale®
& COMPANY

Holidays at Home: Crafts to Celebrate the Season
© 2004 by Martingale & Company

Martingale & Company®
20205 144th Avenue NE
Woodinville, WA 98072-8478
www.martingale-pub.com

Credits

President: Nancy J. Martin

CEO: Daniel J. Martin

Publisher: Jane Hamada

Editorial Director: Mary V. Green

Managing Editor: Tina Cook

Technical Editor: Dawn Anderson

Copy Editor: Mary Martin

Design Director: Stan Green

Illustrators: Laurel Strand and Robin Strobel

Photographer: Bill Lindner

Photo Assistant: Jason Lund

Photo Stylist: Bridget Haugh

Cover and Text Designer: Stan Green

Green package ribbons on pages 10, 11, and 32 and red velvet ribbon on page 83 were provided by Mokuba.

Printed in China
09 08 07 06 05 04   8 7 6 5 4 3 2 1

Library of Congress Cataloging-in-Publication Data

Holidays at home : crafts to celebrate the season.
        p. cm.
    ISBN 1-56477-517-8
1. Christmas decorations. 2. Handicraft.
I. Martingale & Company.
    TT900.C4H645 2004
    745.594'12—dc22

                                    2003027004

Mission Statement

Dedicated to providing quality products
and service to inspire creativity.

CONTENTS

AROUND THE HOUSE
63

INTRODUCTION

Preparing for the holidays is like baking the perfect batch of Christmas cookies—you need the right tools, the finest ingredients, and a hearty dose of holiday spirit. After you have the materials, the process should just be fun! You can enjoy that same kind of fun with *Holidays at Home*. And best of all, you'll end up with beautiful holiday items that will last year after year (unlike that plate of goodies!).

Around the Tree

Almost every family has a tradition when it comes to the Christmas tree. Whether you search out a tree at a local tree farm or pull a memory-filled artificial tree from the attic each year, we've put together a host of new ways to give your tree holiday cheer. Set the foundation for a bounty of gift boxes with a mistletoe tree skirt. Then trim your tree with beaded icicles, sparkling baskets, glittered ball ornaments, and miniature picture frames that highlight favorite family photos.

Around the Table

Make your holiday gatherings memorable for family and friends by dressing up your table with a snowflake table runner, a beaded chandelier garland, and Santa Cat cocktail napkins. Then serve holiday drinks in etched Noel glasses and offer appetizers on an easy-to-stencil holly serving tray.

Around the Home

Every room needs a touch of holiday spirit! In this section, you'll find embroidered hand towels for the bath, beaded candle wreaths for the coffee table, festive painted canvases for the wall, cuffed stockings for the mantel, and a beautiful boxwood wreath for the front door. Spread holiday cheer to your guests with a stenciled welcome mat for the front step.

Embrace the joy your own two hands can bring to the holidays. You'll quickly find yourself in the Christmas spirit—and you'll find that the true gift is in sharing that spirit with those around you.

AROUND
THE TREE

Beaded Baskets

BY DAWN ANDERSON

Create these sparkling gold and silver beaded baskets to add a special touch to your holiday tree. These miniature cone-shaped baskets are accented at the top with gold wire spirals, a beaded border, and a beaded gold handle. A decorative beaded drop hangs from the bottom tip. To make these ornaments, you first will need to construct a wire framework, which can be wrapped with wired lengths of seed beads. The first couple rows of beading take a little patience, but the rest of the beading goes rather quickly.

Materials *(for one basket)*

+ 1 hank of gold or silver-lined size 11 crystal seed beads
+ 1 hank of red silver-lined size 11 seed beads
+ 1 vial of gold seed beads
+ 37 bronze fire-polished beads, size 4 mm
+ 1 ruby fire-polished bead, size 8 mm
+ 1 size .045 round brass rod, 36"
+ 28-gauge gold spool wire
+ 24-gauge gold spool wire
+ Eye pin from 20-gauge wire
+ Head pin from 20-gauge wire
+ Permanent marker
+ Corrugated cardboard scrap (about 2½" square)
+ Double-stick tape
+ Light-colored flannel or wool scrap (about 14" square)
+ Masking tape
+ Pliers: chain-nose, flat-nose, and round-nose
+ Scissors
+ Wire cutters

Instructions

1. Cut three pieces of brass rod, measuring 12" each, with wire cutters. Mark a point on each rod at its center, using a permanent marker. Hold a rod firmly in a pair of flat-nose pliers next to the marked point. Push the rod forward against the tool, using your thumb to make a 90° angle. Move the flat-nose pliers down the rod about ½" and continue to push the other half of the rod forward, stopping before the shape of the side begins to distort. Crimp the folded end between the jaws of the pliers to make a hairpin shape. Repeat the bending process for the remaining two pieces of rod.

2. Holding the rod in a V shape in front of you, grasp one end of the rod in the jaws of a pair of round-nose pliers, and roll it forward to make a loop. Remove the round-nose pliers and then hold the loop in chain-nose pliers. Begin coiling the brass rod around the loop by pressing the rod away from you with your thumb. Keep an even amount of space between the rings of the coil. Open the pliers and move them along the length of the rod in about ⅛" to ¼" increments while coiling. Continue coiling until the size of the coil measures about ⅜" in diameter. Repeat to make coils at both ends of each frame piece.

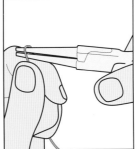

Make loop with round-nose pliers.

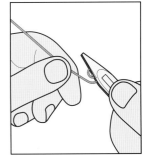

Coil wire around center loop, holding coil with chain-nose pliers.

Bend a slight curve in each half of the brass rod near the coils to match the pattern on page 17 by running the rod between your thumb and forefinger, bending the shape into the rod with your thumb. Continue to shape the frame pieces until the shapes match the patterns on page 17. Note that if you lay your wire frame on the pattern, your coils will be facing up, rather than flat against the page. If your coils are not facing up, bend them up now. To further check the shape, turn your frame piece on its side with the coil flat against the page, check its shape, and make adjustments as necessary. Repeat on the other half of the frame piece.

3. Cut a 20" length of 24-gauge wire. Place two frame pieces flat on a work surface side by side with points facing up. Bind them together near the points with two wraps of the 24-gauge wire. Place the third frame piece on the right of the other two. Carry one end of the 24-gauge wire to the right. Bind the second and third frame pieces together as shown. Raise the frame pieces off the work surface and bring the remaining spokes of the first and third frame pieces together. Bind them together with two wraps of 24-gauge wire; then twist tails together for ⅜" and trim excess.

4. Photocopy or trace the circle pattern on page 17 onto paper. Adhere the paper to the corrugated cardboard with double-stick tape. Cut on the outer marked line with scissors. Place the wire frame pointed side up and position the circle inside the frame, just above the coils. Tape the frame to the circle, aligning each

spoke of the frame with one of the marked lines on the edge of the circle. Trim the eye pin to a length of about 1¼", using the wire cutters. Cup your hand around the wire cutters while cutting to catch loose pieces and prevent them from flying into the air. Position the eye pin at the pointed end of the ornament, with the loop extending ⅛" beyond the point and the remaining length of wire projecting into the interior of the wire frame. Insert the round-nose pliers into the center of the frame, near the point. Bend a small loop in the end of the eye pin and coil it until the wire can be coiled no farther. This is to prevent it from slipping through the pointed end of the frame. Shape the sides of the frame pieces as necessary between your thumb and forefinger to make the shape of each spoke identical for a symmetrical look.

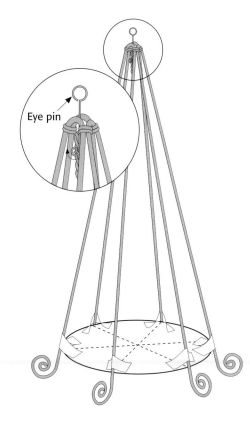

Eye pin

5. Lay a flannel or wool scrap on your work surface to prevent loose beads from rolling. Cut about 30" of 28-gauge wire. Crimp it at one end to prevent beads from coming off. Separate a string of silver or gold seed beads from the hank without removing it from the

hank. Starting at one end of the string, thread the wire through the beads a couple of inches at a time, so that the beads are temporarily threaded through both the string and the wire. Upon reaching the remaining end, push the wire 2" past the last bead on the string. Then, holding tightly to the wire end, remove the string from the hank and transferred beads. Repeat to transfer all but two strings of beads to the wire, cutting additional 30" lengths of wire as necessary and crimping the ends to prevent beads from coming off. Set beaded lengths of wire aside. Remove beads from remaining two strings and lay on flannel or wool scrap to prevent them from rolling away.

6. Cut a 26" length of 28-gauge wire and wrap the end three times around one brass spoke of the frame at its pointed end. Wrap the wire so it passes over the top of the spokes around the frame in the direction you intend to bead. String two or more of the loose beads onto the wire as necessary to reach the wire eye pin. Wrap the wire once around the eye pin. Add two or more beads as necessary to reach and cover the next pair of spokes around the frame that were previously joined with wire.

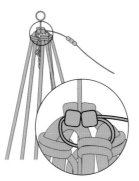

Holding the beads on top of the spokes to prevent slipping, insert the wire to one side of the spokes, then under the spokes, and back up on the other side; pull snug. Insert the wire through the beads sitting on top of the spokes, pull snug, and add more beads to the wire to reach and cover the next pair of spokes. Holding the beads on top of the spokes to prevent slipping, wrap the wire around the pair of spokes and back to the outside; pull snug. Insert the wire into the beads sitting on the

spokes, add more beads, and continue in this manner until you reach a point where the wire can be inserted easily in between each spoke. At this point, add just enough beads to reach the next spoke with the last bead added sitting on top of the spoke. Wrap the wire around just one spoke, add more beads, and continue around the frame until you near the end of the wire. End by wrapping the wire once around a spoke. Wrap the end of a new length of beaded wire around the same spoke. Twist the ends tightly together with the chain-nose pliers and clip the twisted ends to ⅜" long, using the wire cutters. Push the twisted ends to the inside of the ornament. Wrap the beaded wire around the brass frame. At each spoke, spread the beads to expose the wire. Then wrap the wire once around the spoke.

Continue beading in this manner, joining additional lengths of beaded wire as necessary, until you are ½" away from the coils. Remove the cardboard circle as you finish. End around a spoke, and then remove excess seed beads from the wire.

DESIGNER'S TIP

For easier retrieval of the wire once you have inserted it into the frame at the pointed end of the ornament, make a small curve in the end of the wire before you insert it. This way the end naturally curves back to the outside of the frame, allowing you to grab it and pull it through using the chain-nose pliers.

7. To the beading wire, add about 15" of red seed beads. Wrap the beaded wire around the frame with the same technique that you have been using until you complete two rows of beads. Remove any excess beads. To the beading wire, add just enough alternating gold seed beads and bronze fire-polished beads to reach the next spoke. The beaded sequence should fit evenly between the two spokes. If necessary, remove the beads you have just added and rearrange them so that the beaded sequence falls evenly between the two spokes with seed beads filling any gaps on each side. Continue the same sequence of beads between each pair of spokes until you complete one row of bronze and gold beads. Then continue to add two more rows of red seed beads. At the end, wrap the wire tightly back down a spoke, threading it through rows of beaded wires as necessary for about 1"; trim the excess. If coils are too high, continue coiling them down or shape them outward to a desired position. If coils are not tall enough to allow room for the last row of beads, uncoil them slightly.

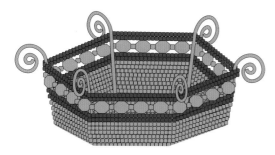

8. Insert a head pin into a bronze bead and then into an 8-mm ruby bead. Trim excess wire about a scant ⅜" above the last bead, using a wire cutter. Grasp the wire in the jaws of the round-nose pliers near the tip and roll the wire forward to make a loop. Remove the round-nose pliers and grab the base of the loop with the chain-nose pliers. Rotate your hand back, bending the loop at a sharp angle. Remove the pliers and reinsert the round-nose pliers into

the loop; rotate forward to make a complete circle and make the beaded drop.

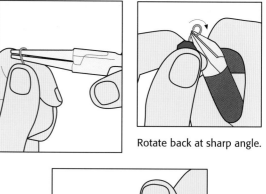

Rotate back at sharp angle.

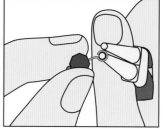

9. Open the loop by grasping half of it in the jaws of chain-nose pliers and rotating it away from you. Do not pull the loop apart to open it or you will distort its round shape. Slip the end of the open loop onto the wire loop at the pointed end of the ornament and close the loop. To close the loop, grasp half of it in the chain-nose pliers and rotate it to a closed position.

10. Cut a 15" length of 24-gauge wire and wrap it around one side of the round-nose pliers to make a loop about 2" from one end. Using your chain-nose pliers, bend the long wire at a 90° angle to the loop. Then wrap the short wire three times around the long wire and trim the excess.

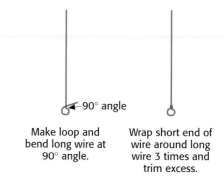

90° angle

Make loop and bend long wire at 90° angle.

Wrap short end of wire around long wire 3 times and trim excess.

11. To make the basket handle, thread five gold seed beads onto the remaining end of the wire, followed by a bronze bead. Repeat this sequence 12 times; then add five more seed beads. Make a loop in wire at the end in the same manner as at the beginning. Slip one of the wire loops onto one coil of the basket, threading it on from the inside of the coil. Slip the wire loop on the remaining end of the handle onto the coil on the opposite side of the basket. If the end of the coil is so tightly coiled that you can't slip the loop onto it, pry it open slightly with the chain-nose pliers. Slip the wire loop into place and return the coil to its original position. Shape the handle as shown.

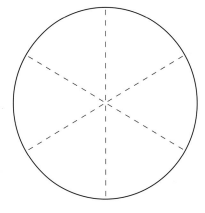

Circle Pattern

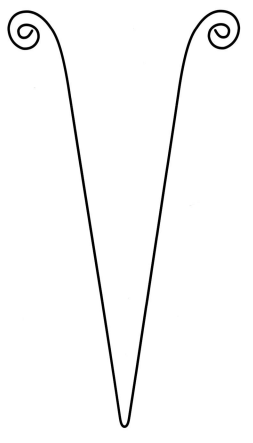

Frame Pattern

Beaded Icicle Ornaments

BY DAWN ANDERSON

These beaded icicles are created by threading an assortment of glass beads and gold bead

caps onto a long hat pin and then forming a loop at the top to add a decorative brass hook.

The large accent beads, most often used at the top of the icicles, are hollow glass Venetian

beads with striped or swirled designs. Although the ornaments appear fragile, they really are

quite durable. Hang them from a tree or a chandelier, or display them in a window.

Materials *(for one ornament)*

- One 6" brass hat pin
- 1 or 2 hollow glass Venetian beads (Beads & Beyond, see "Sources" on page 96)
- 7 to 13 glass beads in 3 to 4 different sizes, ranging from 6 mm to 10 mm
- 2 size 6 seed beads for each Venetian bead
- 2 gold bead caps for each Venetian bead used (should be large enough to cover holes at ends of beads)
- 6" of 16-gauge brass wire
- Pliers: round-nose and chain-nose
- Terry cloth hand towel (white preferred)
- Wire cutters
- ¾" wood dowel

Instructions

1. Fold the terry cloth towel in half, and place it on a work surface to use for arranging beads so they won't roll away. On one side of the towel, separate the beads into groups by size and color. On the other side of the towel, begin arranging beads in a straight line, starting with the Venetian bead at the top. Use the beading diagram (right) as a guide for arranging your beads. (Note: bead caps and seed beads will be added in step 2.) To make an icicle with only one Venetian bead, start arranging the beads from the top down, using large and medium

sizes for the first five to six beads (alternating between sizes if desired), then using medium and small beads for the next five to six beads (alternating between sizes if desired). To make an icicle with two Venetian beads, remove about four continuous beads in the arrangement, close to the first Venetian bead, and replace them with a second Venetian bead.

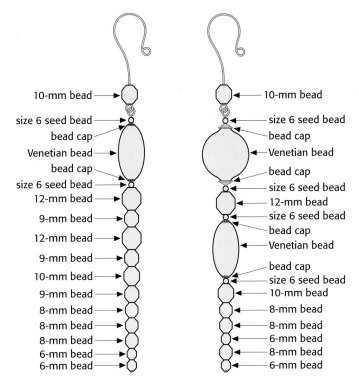

Beading Diagram

2. Begin threading the arrangement of beads onto a brass hat pin, starting with the smaller beads and progressing toward the larger beads. Before threading a Venetian bead onto the pin, first place a bead cap over each hole in the bead. Then add one size 6 seed bead to each side of the bead, next to the bead caps. Thread beads onto the pin in that order. You should have at least ½" remaining on your pin. If not, rearrange or remove a bead as necessary so that you have at least ½" of the pin sticking up beyond the last bead.

3. Trim the end of the pin, removing the sharp point, so that only ⅜" extends up beyond the last bead. Be sure to trim with the point with the pin facing down, cupping your free hand around the end of the pin to catch the loose piece.

4. Grasp the end of the pin in the jaws of the round-nose pliers near the tip and roll forward, creating a loop. Remove the round-nose pliers and grab the base of the loop with the chain-nose pliers as shown. Rotate your hand back, bending the loop back at a sharp angle. Remove the pliers and reinsert the round-nose pliers into the loop as far as they will go and roll forward to make a complete circle that is centered above the pin.

5. To make the hook, grasp one end of the 16-gauge wire in the jaws of the round-nose pliers and roll forward to make a loop. Bend the wire around a dowel close to the loop to make the hook. Trim the wire about 1⅛" from the dowel and remove the dowel. Bend the wire to match the hook pattern below. Insert an accent bead onto the wire. Create a loop in the wire at the bottom of the hook as in step 4.

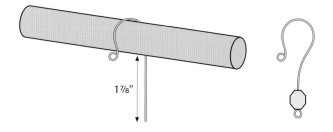

1⅛"

6. Open the bottom loop in the hook by rotating half of the loop forward with chain-nose pliers. Insert the end of the wire loop into the loop of the icicle and then rotate it back to a closed position.

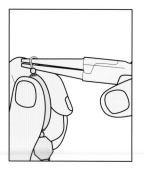 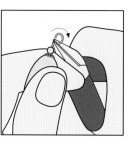

Bend back at sharp angle.

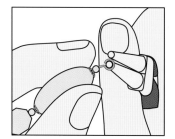

Hook Pattern

COLLAGE FRAME ORNAMENTS

BY SARALYN EWALD, Creative Coordinator, Archiver's: The Photo Memory Store

These miniature frames are the perfect place to display some of your favorite family photos, where they can be enjoyed on your tree year after year. Specific instructions are given to make the ones shown here, but you can customize the frames to your own decor with the papers and embellishments you select.

Materials *(for three frame ornaments)*

TREE FRAME

+ One 4" x 4" piece of printed script paper (Autumn Leaves/7 Gypsies "Livre" paper #1310)
+ One 1" x 2" piece of green tone-on-tone patterned paper (Daisy D's Paper Company–Robin Randolph "Secret Garden" #1815)
+ One 2" x 2" piece of white cardstock
+ Gold oval concho (Scrap Works)
+ 1½"-long silver tree charm with loop (Making Memories Christmas Variety Eyelet Charms)
+ 1"-long brass tree charm
+ 5" of ⅜"-wide olive/brown iridescent ribbon (May Arts #KA08)
+ Marking pen and pencil with eraser

NOEL FRAME

+ One 2" x 4" piece of gold printed mulberry paper
+ One 2" x 4" piece of white cardstock
+ One 4" x 4" piece of textured copper paper
+ Scrap of cardstock (to back NOEL stickers)
+ Rusty metal holly leaves on a vine
+ Four 3-mm copper beads
+ Gold metallic thread (On the Surface New Metallics gold fiber)
+ Black typewriter stickers (Stickopotamus Rebecca Sower Designs—Nostalgiques "Black Typewriter Stickers")
+ Copper pigment ink (Tsukineko, Inc. Dauber Duos)
+ Super-fine detail gold embossing powder (Ranger Industries)

+ Embossing heat tool (Marvy Uchida)
+ Small paintbrush
+ Scrap paper

SNOWFLAKE FRAME

+ One 3" x 4" piece of green tone-on-tone patterned paper (Daisy D's Paper Company–Robin Randolph "Secret Garden Solid" #1815)
+ One 2" x 4" piece of printed black script paper (Autumn Leaves/7 Gypies parchment with black handwriting #1317)
+ Measuring tape sticker (Stickopotamus Rebecca Sower Designs–Nostalgiques "Rule of Thumb" Stickers)
+ Silver snowflake charm (Boutique Trims, Inc. Embellish It! Silver Mixed Snowflake Charms)
+ Silver thread

MATERIALS (FOR ALL FRAMES)

+ 18-gauge copper wire (Anchor Wire)
+ Double-sided dry tacky tape (Suze Weinberg's Wonder Tape)
+ pH neutral PVA bookbinding glue (Books by Hand)
+ Scissors
+ Soft, damp cloth
+ Staple gun and staples
+ Three 3" x 3" metal-wrapped wood (or wood) photo frames
+ Three family photos and access to a photo-copy machine
+ Wire cutters
+ X-Acto knife and self-healing cutting mat

Instructions

1. Remove the frame glass and back from each metal frame. Wipe the surface of each frame to remove any dust.

2. Cover the front of each frame with strips of Wonder Tape, carefully positioning the tape almost flush with each edge.

3. **Tree frame:** Center the 4" x 4" piece of script paper over the front of the frame, covering the center opening. Press to secure; set aside.

   Noel frame: Apply a 2" x 4" piece of white cardstock across the upper 1½" of the frame. Glue the strip of gold-printed mulberry paper over the cardstock, using liquid bookbinding glue. Tear along one side of the textured copper paper square and press the paper onto the lower portion of the frame, overlapping the mulberry paper slightly with the torn edge. Apply a little liquid glue under the torn edge of the copper paper if necessary to secure where the papers overlap. Set aside.

   Snowflake frame: Apply the 3" x 4" piece of green paper to the top half of the frame and the black script paper to the bottom half of the frame. Then apply the measuring tape sticker over the join line, just below the middle of the frame.

4. Turn each frame over and cut off the excess paper with an X-Acto knife, using the outer-edge of the frame as a guide.

5. Cut out the paper covering the window of each frame with an X-Acto knife, following the inside edge of the window as a guide.

6. Cut three 10" lengths of copper wire. Bend and shape the wire into hangers, using the patterns on page 24 as a guide and wrapping the wire around the barrel of a pen to create smooth loops.

7. Use a staple gun to attach the shaped copper wire to the back of each frame as shown.

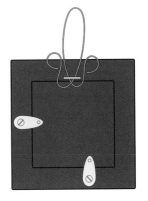

8. **Tree frame:** Tear the edges around the 1" x 2" piece of green paper so it fits within the width of the frame, centered above the window opening. Secure it in place with Wonder Tape. Trace around the oval concho onto the 2" square of white cardstock and trim just inside the marked line so that the cardstock fits inside the oval concho. Write the date or name as desired on the paper, insert it into the concho and press down the prongs on the back side using the eraser end of a pencil. Tie the ribbon in a knot through the loop in the top of the silver tree charm and trim ends of the ribbon at angles. Adhere the metal tree charms and concho to the front of the frame as shown in the photo, using small strips of Wonder Tape.

Noel frame: Cut about a 2" strip of metal holly leaves on a vine, using a wire cutter, and bend in an arc to fit in the upper left corner of the frame; secure with liquid bookbinding glue. Thread two beads onto gold thread and tie in a knot. Trim the ends. Repeat with a second pair of beads. Apply a drop of bookbinding glue to the frame along the vine and position a bead cluster in the middle of the drop. Repeat with the second cluster and let dry. Dab rubber-stamping ink around the edge of each of the NOEL stickers. Apply embossing powder to the ink and remove excess powder with a small paintbrush. Lightly stick the letters to a piece of scrap paper and use a heat gun to melt the embossing powder. Remove the stickers from the paper and back each one with a small circle of cardstock to give the sticker some height. Glue the stickers to the frame as shown in the photo with bookbinding glue.

Snowflake frame: Tie a 5" piece of silver thread through the loop of the snowflake charm and tie in a bow. Trim excess. Adhere the snowflake charm to the upper right corner of the frame using a small piece of Wonder Tape.

9. Put the glass back inside each frame. Use a photocopier to copy and size photos to fit inside each frame opening. Trim photos to size and insert into frames. Replace the back on each frame to secure the glass and photos inside.

Hanger Patterns

COPPER ORNAMENTS

BY TRACY STANLEY

Create these charming, rustic ornaments with copper sheet, some copper wire, beads, and charms. Add stamped designs and Christmas messages using steel alphabet marking tools and decorative metal stamps.

Materials *(for the three ornaments)*

+ Three 6" x 6" copper sheets
+ Steel alphabet marking tool set (I used sets of different sizes to vary the size of my letters.)
+ 18-gauge copper wire
+ Metal stamps in assorted designs (spirals, stars, moons, dots, zigzags, etc.)
+ About 30 assorted beads for star and moon ornaments
+ About 30 size 6 seed beads for tree ornament
+ 3 long gold eye pins
+ Star charms:
  • Two ⅜" for tree-shaped ornament
  • One ⅜", one ½", and one ¾" for moon-shaped ornament
+ Scissors
+ Rubber cement
+ Tin snips
+ Ball peen hammer
+ Steel bench block
+ Metal file
+ Masking tape
+ Block of wood
+ Awl or nail
+ Wire cutters
+ Pliers: round-nose and chain-nose
+ Measuring cup
+ Microwave
+ Liver of sulfur (optional)
+ Plastic forks
+ Paper towels
+ 0000 steel wool
+ Polishing cloth

Instructions

1. Photocopy or trace the ornament patterns on pages 28–29 onto paper and cut them out. Glue them to a copper sheet. Let dry, and then cut around pattern lines, using the tin snips.

2. To texturize the outer edges of each ornament, place the ornament on top of the steel block and pound the edges of the ornament with the rounded end of the ball peen hammer. Work around the entire edge of each ornament. File down any sharp edges.

3. Using the masking tape, tape the ornament to the steel block to keep the metal from jumping when you stamp your words. Referring to the photo for placement, use the steel alphabet marking tools and the ball peen hammer to stamp "AND TO ALL A GOOD NIGHT" on the moon and tree ornaments. Stamp "MERRY CHRISTMAS" on the star ornament, using letters of different sizes if desired. For a whimsical look, place the letters freehand, or for perfect alignment use a ruler as a guide.

DESIGNER'S TIP

You may want to practice your stamping on a scrap piece of metal. Be sure to hold the stamp firmly and straight up and down. Strike once, firmly, with the hammer. If you hit the stamp more than once it may cause a shadowing effect.

4. Using the hammer and the decorative metal stamps, add designs such as stars, moons, swirls, and zigzags to the ornaments.

5. Place an ornament on the piece of wood. Using the hammer, tap the awl or nail at the top of the ornament to create a hole for hanging as indicated on the pattern. Repeat for each ornament. Add four more holes on the tree, three on the moon, and one on the star as indicated on the patterns. File the sharp edges on the back of the ornaments.

6. Cut a 9" length of wire, using a wire cutter. Insert the wire into a hole at the top of an ornament, stopping at midpoint in the wire. Slide a couple of beads onto the front wire if desired. Fold the wire in half and twist the halves tightly together. Trim the end. Grasp the end in the jaws of a pair of round-nose pliers and roll it forward to make a loop. Shape the remainder of the wire into a hook shape, using the pattern on page 28 as a guide. Repeat for each ornament.

7. **Star ornament:** Cut a 5" length of copper wire. Grasp the end of the wire in the jaws of round-nose pliers near the tip and coil it forward three times, removing and reinserting the pliers as necessary to make the coil. Bend the remaining end at a 90° angle to the coil, using the chain-nose pliers.

Thread about seven beads onto the end of the wire. Just above the beads, wrap the wire around one side of the round-nose pliers to make a loop. Trim the excess wire. Slip the loop into the hole at the bottom of the star ornament.

Moon ornament: Thread six to eight beads onto each eye pin. Just above the beads, wrap the eye-pin wire around one side of the round-nose pliers to make a loop. Trim the excess. Slip the loop into a hole at the bottom of the moon ornament. Grasp half the loop at the end of the eye pin in the chain-nose pliers and rotate your hand forward to open the loop. Slip a ⅜" star charm onto the loop. Grasp half the loop in the chain-nose pliers again and rotate your hand back to close the loop. Repeat for the remaining two eye pins, using a ½" star charm for one and a ¾" star charm for the other.

Tree ornament: Cut a 15" length of copper wire. Grasp one end in the jaws of the round-nose pliers and roll it forward to make a loop. Remove the round-nose pliers; then hold the loop in the jaws of the chain-nose pliers. Begin coiling the wire around the loop by pressing the wire away from you using your thumb. Make a tight coil about ⅜" in diameter.

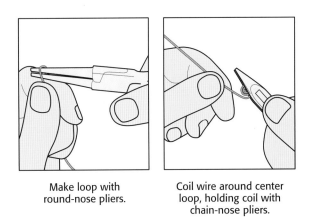

Make loop with round-nose pliers.

Coil wire around center loop, holding coil with chain-nose pliers.

Add a couple of size 6 beads to the wire and then coil the wire around one side of the round-nose pliers a couple of times. Add another bead and coil the wire some more. Continue alternating between coiling wire and adding beads to make a length about 2". Then thread the wire through a hole at the bottom of the tree from the front side. Bring the end back around to the front and continue adding beads and coils as before until you reach the next hole. Insert the wire from front to back in the second hole. Then bring the wire back around to the front and continue adding beads and coiling for about 2" more. Trim the wire 1½" from the end and make a ⅜"-diameter coil as before. Press and shape the coiled wire to follow the tree's contours along the lower edge, around the corners, and up the sides for about 1". Pry open the two copper jump rings and insert them into the remaining holes in the tree. Thread the ⅜" star charms onto the rings, and then close the rings.

8. Heat a cup of water to boiling in the microwave. Remove the water from the microwave, and then add a chunk of liver of sulfur. Submerse the ornaments in the mixture until they begin to turn black. Remove the ornaments with forks, rinse off with water, and pat dry with paper towels. Rub the front of the ornaments with steel wool, leaving black in the recessed design areas. Polish with a polishing cloth for a nice finish.

DESIGNER'S TIP

Liver of sulfur has an odor similar to rotten eggs. Work with it outdoors. Instead of liver of sulfur, you could also highlight the decorative stamped images with black metal paint. Quickly brush the paint over the stamped designs and rub off immediately with a paper towel, leaving paint in the recessed areas. The copper will age with time.

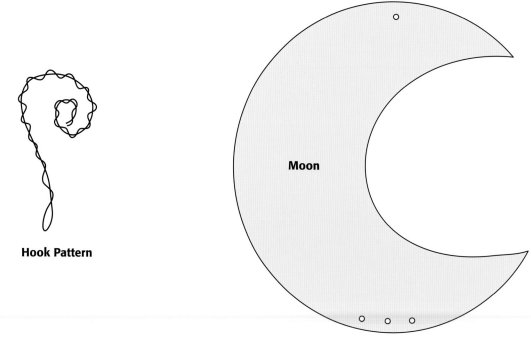

Hook Pattern

Moon

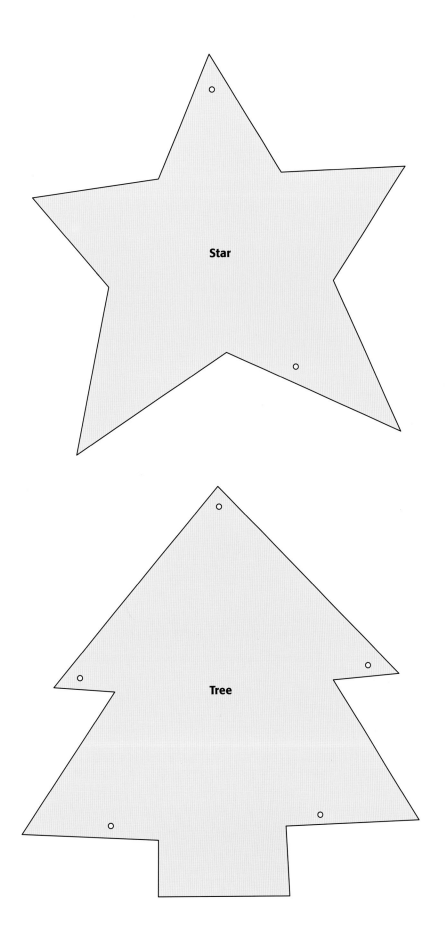

Star

Tree

GLITTERED BALL ORNAMENTS

BY LIVIA McREE

Dress up your tree with these sparkling glitter and rhinestone ornaments. There are only three simple steps to making these eye-catching decorations: simply draw the design onto the ornament with a glue bottle, sprinkle with glitter, and accent with rhinestones. Drawing on a curved surface with a glue bottle naturally produces varying results from ornament to ornament, adding whimsical charm to the designs.

Materials

+ Green and red satin glass ball ornaments
+ Ultrafine opaque white glitter (Barbara Trombley's Original Art Glittering System, Angel Dust)
+ Flat-backed rhinestones (Westrim Crafts):
  - 4½-mm peridot
  - 3-mm ruby
+ Access to a photocopy machine
+ Scissors
+ Mini double-sided adhesive dots (Glue Dots)
+ Clear adhesive and ultra-fine metal tip (The Art Glittering System Dries Clear Adhesive)
+ Scrap paper
+ Pencil with eraser
+ Large blunt-end darning needle
+ Several 2" or 3" sections of a paper towel tube
+ Tweezers

Instructions

1. Photocopy the patterns (right) onto paper, reducing or enlarging as desired to fit your ornaments. Cut out around both the solid and dotted lines of the pattern. Apply Glue Dots directly to the backs of the pattern pieces in several places. Lightly adhere one pattern piece to the center front of one ornament as best you can. It won't fit smoothly.

2. Fit the metal tip on the adhesive bottle. Draw on the ornament around the solid pattern outline (not the dotted line) with the glue bottle; use the darning needle to finesse the outline by smoothing out the glue, if necessary. It is okay if the outline is thick.

3. With a piece of paper as your work surface, sprinkle glitter over the adhesive. Then tap off the excess. Use the paper to funnel the extra glitter back into the container. Set the ornament on a section of paper towel tube so that it will dry without rolling around.

4. Once the ornament is dry, remove the pattern. Then scribble a little bit of adhesive inside your design. Use the end of a pencil eraser to spread the glue around in a thin layer. Sprinkle glitter on the ornament as in step 3; let dry.

5. Use small drops of adhesive and a pair of tweezers to attach the rhinestones to the tips of the tree branches and along the top of the stocking and bottom of the mitten as shown in the photo on page 30. Sprinkle a bit of glitter over them if any glue squeezes out around the edges.

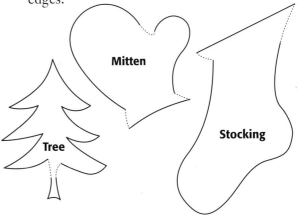

Mitten

Tree

Stocking

MISTLETOE APPLIQUÉ TREE SKIRT

BY GENEVIEVE A. STERBENZ

This distinctive Christmas tree skirt is decorated with a delicate arrangement of no-sew appliqué mistletoe leaves, pearl berries, ribbon, and rickrack trim. Wool flannel in pale green provides the background color for this elegant tree skirt. Soft shades of light and medium green for the appliqués, trims, and lining create a monochromatic palette.

Materials

- 1¾ yards of pale gray-green wool flannel, 60" wide
- ¼ yard of medium green wool felt or flannel
- 1¾ yards of lining fabric in a coordinating color
- 46 cream pearl beads, 14 mm
- 6⅛ yards of green rickrack, 2" wide
- 6⅛ yards of light green grosgrain ribbon, ¼" wide
- Thread in a coordinating color
- Hand-sewing needle
- Straight pins
- Beading thread
- Fabric glue
- Thumbtack
- Chalk pencil
- Masking tape
- Spray adhesive
- 8 Velcro self-adhesive dots
- Small square of corrugated cardboard
- Newspaper
- Iron and ironing board
- Scissors
- Sewing machine
- Sewing shears
- Tape measure with a metal end with a hole in it

Instructions

1. Press the wool fabrics and lining fabric flat using an iron. Set the lining fabric and medium green wool aside. Lay the lighter wool flannel on a clean, flat work surface. To find the center of the largest possible circle, lift one corner of the fabric and fold it over toward the opposite corner so that adjacent sides align, creating a triangle. There will be leftover fabric extending from this triangle. Cut away excess fabric. Fold the triangle in half, matching points. The top center point is the center of the fabric. Mark this center point using

DESIGNER'S TIP

If you cannot find wool felt in the color you want, you can make your own wool felt by machine washing wool in hot water. Dry it in the machine; then iron it with steam to remove wrinkles.

straight pins on both the front and back of the fabric.

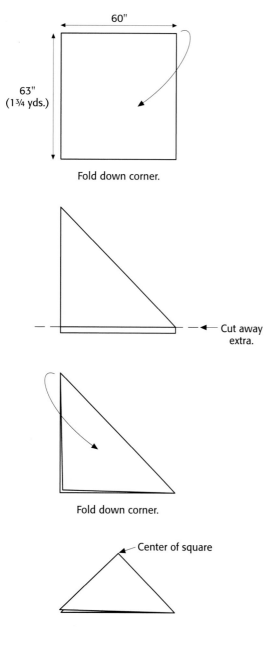

60"

63"
(1¾ yds.)

Fold down corner.

◄— Cut away
extra.

Fold down corner.

◄— Center of square

2. Unfold the fabric, wrong side up, and smooth it flat. Place a small square of cardboard over the center point and secure it in place with some masking tape. Do not worry about the tape ruining the fabric; the center will eventually be cut away, and the lining will cover this side, as well. Turn the fabric to the right side. Tape down the corners of the fabric to secure them. They, too, will be cut away. Create a compass by pushing a thumbtack through the end of the tape measure, into the center point of the fabric, and into the cardboard. Extend the tape measure. Measure and mark three points, using a chalk pencil: one point at 4", one at 27", and one at 28". Continue to move the tape measure and mark these points around the entire square of fabric, creating three circles. Using a ruler and the chalk pencil, mark one straight line from the center of the circle to one point along the outer edge of the circle. Cut along the outside 28" marked line, discarding the excess fabric. The 27" circle will be the stitching line. Then cut along the straight line to the center of the circle and cut away the center circle, cutting along the 4" marked line. The center circle will create the hole for the Christmas tree trunk. Using pins, measure and mark a ½" seam allowance on each edge of the straight line cut to the center of the fabric. Repeat these steps to cut out the lining fabric. Set both fabrics aside.

3. Photocopy or trace the mistletoe patterns on page 36. Cut 10 double leaves and 26 single leaves from the medium green flannel, using sewing shears. Place the light green wool flannel right side up on a clean flat work surface with the center front (opposite the cut line) most accessible. Pin all the leaves in place as shown in the placement diagram on page 36. Each leaf should be 2" from the seam line (the 27" circle) with about 2" between leaf groupings. Lift off one leaf at a time and place it wrong side up on clean newspaper. Apply a light coat of spray adhesive, turn it right side

up and return it to its original position, pressing down to make sure it adheres. Repeat these steps around the entire skirt to adhere all appliqués. Then go over each appliqué with the iron.

DESIGNER'S TIP

Before removing the appliqués to apply the spray adhesive, place a few pins around the outside of the leaves to mark their places.

4. With wool flannel right side up, begin at the back of the skirt and pin the rickrack along the outer edge, with the center of the rickrack on the seam line as shown below. Pin around the entire outer edge of the circle, trimming rick rack even with the cut edge at the center back. Turn up ½" at each end. Pin another length of rickrack along one straight edge at the back of the tree skirt. At the outer edge, turn up ½" at end along the seam line. Then machine stitch in place through the center of the rickrack, removing pins as you work.

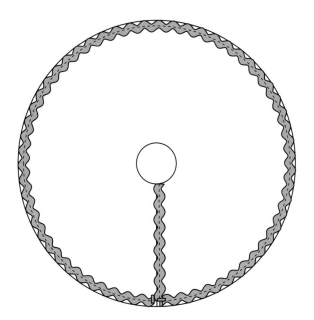

5. Pin the pale green wool and lining, right sides together, with raw edges even. Make sure fabrics are flat, and pin fabrics together around the center as well to prevent slipping. Machine stitch around the outer edges along the seam line and along the opening that has rickrack attached. Stitch around the center circle and partially down the remaining straight side, using a ½" seam allowance, and leaving a large opening for turning. Trim close to the stitching line around curved seams. Notch the fabric around the outer curve and clip around the inner curve. Clip excess fabric from the corners. Turn the tree skirt to its right side, flattening the seams and pushing out the corner fabric.

6. Thread a hand-sewing needle with beading thread and slip the hand that is holding the needle inside the opening of the skirt. Stitch the beads in place as shown in the diagram on page 36.

7. Turn in the raw edges along the opening and slipstitch them closed. Edge stitch around the center hole, using the sewing machine. Use fabric glue to adhere the ¼" grosgrain ribbon around the outer edge of the tree skirt just above the rickrack, beginning and ending at the center back seam; trim the ribbon ⅜" beyond the edges and turn the ends under, gluing them in place. Apply the grosgrain ribbon around the center hole in the same manner. Adhere the loop side of the Velcro dots along the underside of the rickrack trim at the back edge of the tree skirt, placing the dots about 4½" apart, or on every other bump. Adhere the hook side of the Velcro dots on the right side of the tree skirt along the remaining back edge about ⅛" from the edge, so that they align with the loop dots.

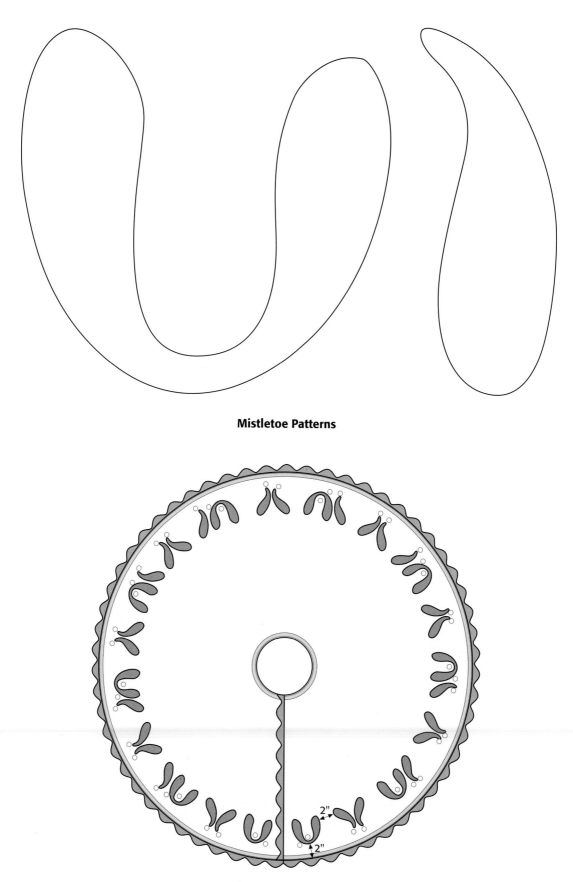

Mistletoe Patterns

Placement Diagram

AROUND THE TABLE

CHRISTMAS CAT COCKTAIL NAPKINS

BY SHEILA HAYNES RAUEN

Create these whimsical Santa Cat cocktail napkins to enjoy during the holidays or to give as a gift. The hand painting is easy to do. Simply trace the design directly onto a ready-made linen napkin and fill in between the lines with the chosen color of paint. The painted designs are then heat set to make the napkins both washable and dry cleanable.

Materials

+ Set of 6 white linen cocktail napkins
+ Jacquard Neopaque Paints in the following colors: Green, Red, Yellow, and Black
+ Jacquard Flowable Extender
+ Waxed paper
+ Paper and pencil or access to a photocopy machine
+ Tape
+ Pencil
+ Iron and ironing board
+ Light box or sunlit window
+ Paintbrushes (Loew-Cornell):
  • American Painter Series 4350 Liner #00
  • Series 797-F Flat Stain size #2

DESIGNER'S TIPS

+ Mix all paints with flowable extender to improve the flow of the paint.

+ Practice painting on a scrap of linen fabric first to hone your painting skills.

+ Clean your brushes after working with each color of paint.

Instructions

1. Wash the napkins to remove sizing. Press them while they are damp. Trace or photocopy the pattern on page 40 onto paper. Tape the pattern to a light box or sunlit window and tape the napkin on top, centering it over the pattern. Trace the pattern onto the napkin using a pencil.

2. Place a piece of waxed paper on your work surface. Then place the marked napkin on the waxed paper. Using the liner brush in the border, paint the vines and holly leaves green.

3. Using the liner brush, paint the holly berries in the border red.

4. Mix a small amount of yellow and green paint to make lime green for the cat's eyes. Referring to the color plan on page 40, paint the eyes lime green, using the liner brush.

5. Referring to the color plan on page 40, paint the cat's body black. Use the liner brush for the small areas and the flat brush for the larger areas. Leave the white areas unpainted. To create the outline around the legs, paint on the pencil lines and then again just to one side of them, leaving three fine white lines to separate the legs from the body. Paint the details of the cat's face and body, such as the eyes, nose, mouth, and paws, using the liner brush.

6. Paint the cat's hats red, using the flat brush. Outline the white areas of the hats using black paint and the liner brush. Allow the paint to dry.

7. Using the liner brush, paint the vine and holly leaves around the cat's neck green. Paint the holly berries red. Allow to dry for 24 hours.

8. Set your iron on the linen setting. Heat set the paint by pressing the napkin with the iron for 30 seconds on each side.

Color Plan

Cocktail Napkin Pattern

ETCHED NOEL GLASSES

BY LIVIA McREE

Add a frosty holiday greeting to plain red glassware by using glass etching crème. Use the patterns included or create your own label designs on a computer, varying the font style for each letter of the word. The instructions below are for cutting a template from adhesive vinyl. You will need to cut an adhesive template for each glass that you etch. To save time when etching several glasses to give as gifts, consider ordering custom-cut stencils from Etchall. (See "Sources" on page 96.)

Materials

+ Red glass tumblers
+ Clear adhesive vinyl or custom stencil
+ Etchall glass etching crème
+ Permanent marker (fine line)
+ Lint-free rag
+ Access to a photocopy machine
+ Masking tape
+ Sponge brush applicator
+ Craft knife
+ Rubber gloves
+ Self-healing cutting mat

Instructions

1. Determine the size of the etching pattern best suited to your glasses by photocopying the oval and the letters (right) at various sizes.

2. Once you decide on the size, tape the pattern to a self-healing cutting mat. Tape a piece of clear adhesive vinyl over the pattern, with the vinyl side facing up (otherwise the letters will be backwards). Using a permanent marker with a fine line, trace the oval and letters.

3. Use a craft knife to cut the oval and letters out of the vinyl, making sure not to cut into the patterns (red areas at right).

4. Wash and dry the glass with a lint-free rag. Try not to get fingerprints where it is to be etched.

5. Firmly press the vinyl pattern pieces to the glass. For quick and easy placement, tape a copy of the pattern to the inside of the glass to serve as a guide. Apply masking tape around the outer edges of the oval pattern to prevent crème from spilling over pattern onto glass.

6. Put on rubber gloves. Following the manufacturer's directions, apply a thick, even layer of crème to the glass over the oval design with a sponge brush applicator. Wait five minutes. Use the applicator to scrape off as much of the crème as possible and then put the crème back in the bottle. Rinse off the remaining crème under warm running water. Remove the vinyl pattern and tape. Wash the glass.

Etched Glasses Patterns

PAINTED CERAMIC SNOWMEN MUGS

BY SHEILA HAYNES RAUEN

Enjoy your favorite hot drink in these wintry mugs. Each of the four mugs is painted with a snowman wearing a different hat. Create one of each as shown here or choose your favorite and make four alike. These mugs were painted with Delta PermEnamel Paints, which after a 10-day curing period are microwave-safe and oven-safe up to 350°, and dishwasher-safe with mild soap.

Materials

+ 4 blue ceramic mugs
+ Delta PermEnamel Surface Conditioner
+ Delta PermEnamel Paints in the following colors: Black, White, Red, Yellow, and Pine Green
+ Delta PermEnamel Satin Glaze or Gloss Glaze
+ Newsprint
+ Tracing paper and pencil
+ Loew-Cornell Superchaco transfer paper
+ Tape
+ Paintbrushes (Loew-Cornell):
  • American Painter Series 4350 Liner #00 and #18/0 Liner
  • Series 797-F Flat Stain sizes #2 and #4

Instructions

1. Wash and dry the mugs to remove dirt or oils that may prevent adhesion of the paints. Cover your work surface with newsprint. Using the #4 flat brush, apply the surface conditioner to the mugs by brushing a coat onto the side of the mug you intend to paint. Note: Paint must be applied within four hours of using the surface conditioner. If more time passes, reapply the surface conditioner and let it dry.

DESIGNER'S TIP

Clean your brushes after working with each color of paint.

2. Trace the patterns on page 46 for the snowman, including the face and button details and the branch arms, onto tracing paper. Trace the desired hats onto smaller pieces of tracing paper (you will need a piece of tracing paper for each style of hat you plan to use), including the dashed line indicating the shape of the snowman's head. These will be used as overlays later to trace the hats onto the painted snowmen.

3. Cut a small piece of transfer paper to fit the tracing of the snowman. Position the tracing paper over the side of the mug you intend to paint, with the transfer paper beneath it transfer side down, and tape in place.

4. Lightly trace the shape of the snowman and the branch arms onto the surface of the mug using a pencil. Remove the tracing and transfer papers. Note: It is possible that the transferred lines may bleed through the paint. This can be corrected by painting over these areas after the first coat of paint has dried.

5. Paint the branch arms of the snowman black, using the #00 liner brush. Paint the snowman's

head and body white, using the #2 flat brush. Let the paint dry.

6. Reposition the tracing and transfer paper over the painted snowman and trace the face details and the buttons onto the surface. Remove the papers. Paint the eyes and buttons black, using the #00 liner brush. Paint the mouth black, using the #18/0 liner brush.

7. Mix a small amount of red paint into the yellow paint to create an orange color for the nose. Paint the nose orange with the #18/0 liner brush. Allow it to dry.

8. Place the overlay for the hat in position (aligning the dashed line with the painted head of the snowman) with the transfer paper beneath, and trace the hat onto the head of the snowman. Remove the tracing and transfer papers.

9. Refer to the color plans (right). For Hat 1, paint the vine and the holly leaves pine green, using the liner brushes. Allow it to dry. For Paint the holly berries red, using the #18/0 liner brush. For Hat 2, paint the evergreen bough pine green, using the #18/0 liner brush.

10. For Hat 3, paint the upper part and brim of the top hat black, using the #2 flat brush. Paint the band of the top hat red, using the #00 liner brush. Allow it to dry. Paint green dots on the band, using the #18/0 liner brush.

11. For Hat 4, paint the hat red, using the #2 flat brush. Allow it to dry. Paint the white details on the hat using the #18/0 liner brush as shown.

12. Paint white dots in the background of the mug around each snowman, using the #18/0 liner brush. Note: If more than 4 hours have passed since you applied the surface conditioner, apply it again before you add the dots to the background.

13. Allow the paint to dry for one hour. Apply the satin glaze or gloss glaze over all the painted areas. Allow the paint to cure for 10 days before washing.

Hat 1

Hat 2

Hat 3

Hat 4

Color Plans

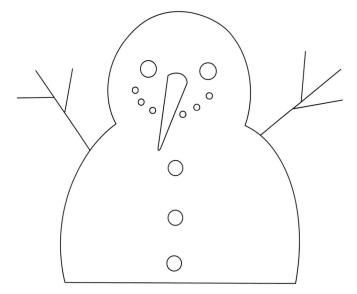

Snowman

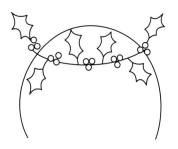

Hat 1
Holly and Berries

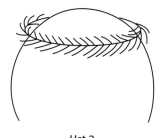

Hat 2
Pine

Hat 3
Top Hat

Hat 4
Knit Cap

Painted Mug Patterns

BEADED SNOWFLAKE
TABLE RUNNER

BY GENEVIEVE A. STERBENZ

Simple sewing is all that is required to bring this elegant runner to your table. Silver beads are sewn on ice blue velvet to create the appearance of a fresh winter snowfall. Snowflakes, in large and small sizes, are hand stitched using silver beads in a variety of shapes and sizes. Although this project may look complicated, it is really very easy because it does not involve any advanced beading techniques.

Materials *(for a 16" x 60" table runner)*

+ 2 yards of blue cotton velveteen
+ 2 yards of blue rayon lining
+ 4 silver flat floral spacers, 6 mm
+ 4 crystal flat-backed rhinestones, 4-mm diameter
+ 2 crystal flat-backed rhinestones, 6-mm diameter
+ 2 hanks of prestrung silver bugle beads, 2 mm x 4.5 mm
+ 2 packages of 4-mm silver pearl beads
+ 2 packages of 9-mm silver teardrop beads
+ Beading needle
+ Coordinating beading thread
+ Fabri-Tac Permanent Adhesive (Beacon)
+ Chalk pencil
+ Straight pins
+ Clear grid ruler
+ Iron and ironing board
+ Scissors
+ Sewing machine
+ Sewing shears

DESIGNER'S TIP

When adding the 4-mm silver beads to the entire length of the velvet, be sure not to sew the beads too close to the marked hem line because this also is your sewing line.

Instructions

1. Press the velveteen and lining fabrics with an iron. Measure, mark, and cut a 17" x 61" rectangle from both the velveteen and the lining fabric. Set the lining fabric aside.

2. Place the velveteen rectangle right side up on a clean work surface. Using a chalk pencil and a grid ruler, measure and mark a ½" hem on all sides. Turn the rectangle so that one width of the fabric is the most accessible.

3. Using straight pins, mark a point on the velveteen 8½" from the left edge and 4" from the bottom edge of the fabric. This point is the center of the largest snowflake. Using the ruler and pins, mark a horizontal line all the way across the velveteen, 4" from the bottom short edge. Then mark a 10" vertical line 8½" from the left edge of the fabric. Use these pinned

lines as a guide to keep the beaded arms of the snowflake straight.

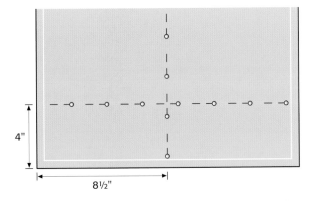

4. Thread the beading needle with a 40" length of thread and knot the ends together. Sew one 6-mm flat-backed rhinestone on the point marked in step 2, for the center of the large snowflake. Using the horizontal pinned line as a guide, follow the beading diagram on page 51 to sew the right and left long arms of the large snowflake, removing pins as you go. Then use the vertical pinned line as a guide to sew the center top and bottom long arms of the snowflake, removing pins as you go. Lay the ruler across the space between the long top and right arm and pin mark the midpoint. Mark a line with pins from the pin mark to the center rhinestone between the two arms of the snowflake. Use this line as a guide for placement of the beads along the short arm. Repeat these steps to create the remaining three short arms between pairs of long arms. Then, using straight pins, measure and mark eight points, ⅝" from the center rhinestone, in between each arm, and sew one teardrop bead at each point as indicated in the diagram.

5. Using the long left arm of the larger snowflake as a guide, measure 1" from the teardrop bead at the end of the arm. Mark this point with a pin. Follow the beading diagram to sew on the two teardrop beads at the end of the arm of the smaller snowflake. Bead along the pinned horizontal line toward the center, following the beading diagram and removing pins as you go. At the center, sew on one flat floral spacer.

Then, glue one 4-mm flat rhinestone in the center of the spacer. Continue working along the horizontal pinned line to the left. Measure and mark another vertical line 3½" from the left edge. Use this line as a guide to create the center top and bottom arms of the smaller snowflake. Lay the ruler between the top and right arm, and pin mark the midpoint. Mark a line with pins from the pin mark to the center rhinestone between the two arms of the snowflake. Use this line as a guide to add another arm of the snowflake. Repeat the process to add the remaining three arms.

6. Bead the smaller right snowflake in the same manner as the left snowflake in step 4. Simply work off the long right horizontal arm of the center snowflake, again measuring 1" from the last bead to begin this snowflake.

7. Turn the velveteen around to the opposite short side and repeat steps 3–6.

8. Turn the velveteen so that one long side is most accessible. Referring to the placement diagram, use pins to mark three points that divide the velveteen into four 15"-long sections. Do not include the seam allowances in these measurements. Repeat these marks on the opposite long side. Begin with one of the 15" sections that include the beaded snowflakes. Sew on 4-mm silver pearl beads randomly, spacing them about 1" apart until you come to about 1" away from the next marked section. In the next section, you will space the 4-mm silver pearl beads 3" apart. To create a blended look between these two sections, space the beads about 1½" to 2" apart along the horizontal line dividing the two sections. Continue beading until you have completed the first two sections. Turn to the opposite side and repeat in the same manner for the remaining two sections of the velveteen.

9. Position and pin the velveteen and the lining, right sides together, with raw edges even. Make sure fabrics are flat and pin both fabrics together in the center as well to prevent slip-

ping. Machine stitch a ½" seam around out-side edges, leaving a 7" opening on one long side for turning; remove pins as you go. Clip excess fabric from the corners and turn the fabric to the right side, flattening seams and making neat corners. Add 4-mm silver beads to any areas near the seam that look bare, using the opening for access. Turn in the remaining edges and hand stitch the opening closed.

10. To add the beaded edging, begin at a short end. At one corner, sew one 4-mm silver pearl bead, followed by a row of bugle beads. To attach the bugle beads, insert your needle up through the fabric at 1, through the bead, down through the fabric at 2, back up at 1 and through the same bead again. Insert the needle through another bead, then down at 3, up at 2 and back through the same bead again. Continue in this manner across the entire width of the runner, stitching through the top layer only. Finish with a silver pearl bead at the opposite corner. Directly above this row of beads, create another row with the pearls and bugle beads identical to the first. Turn to opposite short side and repeat.

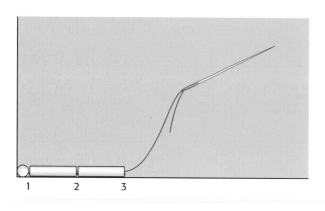

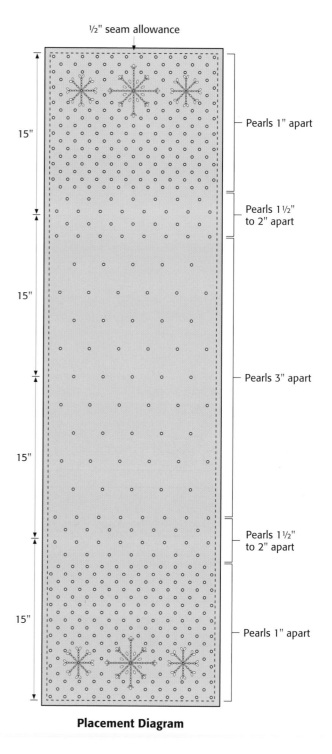

Placement Diagram

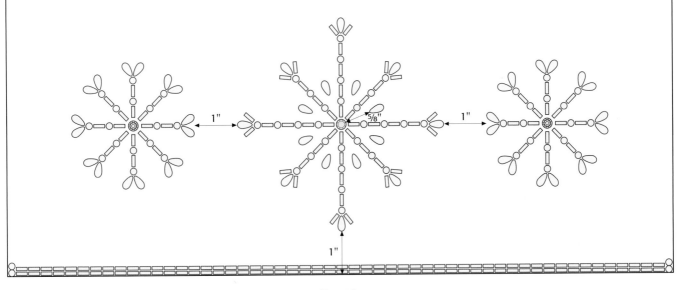

Beading Diagram

◐ 9-mm teardrop	○ 4-mm silver pearl	◉ 6-mm rhinestone
▭ bugle bead	◉ 6-mm flat spacer	◉ 4-mm rhinestone

BEAD-DRAPED CANDLE CHANDELIER

BY DAWN ANDERSON

Drape a light fixture with garlands of green and red glass beads and family photos to create a cherished holiday accent. A candle chandelier was used here, but this would also work on a dining room light fixture that has five arms. Each of the photos was photocopied and sized to fit perfectly into the mini frame tags. In addition to beads and photos, add a few sprigs of cedar and some artificial berries to create the finishing touch.

Materials

- 10 photos and access to a photocopy machine
- Cardstock paper
- 10 large oval metal photo frame tags (Nunn Design)
- 18-gauge gold spool wire
- 20-gauge gold spool wire
- ¼"-diameter rod, such as a knitting needle or nail
- 215 red, smooth, round pressed-glass beads, 10 mm
- 6 red, smooth, round pressed-glass beads, 14 mm
- 6 red, smooth, round pressed-glass beads, 18 mm
- Two 6" vials of size 6 green seed beads
- 6 green spiral beads, 6 mm x 25 mm
- Pencil or chalk pencil
- Double-sided adhesive tape
- ¾"-wide double-sided super tape (Therm O Web)
- Pliers: round-nose, chain-nose, and flat-nose
- Scissors

DESIGNER'S TIPS

- Since I started with a gold fixture, I used gold-colored wire, gold bell caps, and gold frame tags to assemble my beaded garlands and beaded drops. Take into consideration the color of your light fixture and select wire, bell caps, and frame tags in colors that match or coordinate with it. Although wire is available in a variety of colors, bead caps are usually found in the three basic metal colors of silver, gold, and copper.

- All light fixtures vary in their construction. As long you can easily wrap wire around the arms under the light or candleholder and around the center in some way, you should be able to drape it with beads. You can also decorate a chandelier that has three, four, or six arms as well.

Instructions

1. Photocopy your photos onto cardstock, sizing the images to fit inside the frame tags. Remove one of the paper ovals from one of the frame tags to use as a template. Hold your photo up to a light, placing the frame behind the photo, with the image centered in the oval. Then place the oval paper template over your image, centering the oval paper over the oval shadow of the tag. Holding the template over the image, carefully lay the image on a flat work surface and trace around it with a pencil or chalk pencil. Cut just inside the marked line.

2. Secure the image to the center of the frame tag, using double-sided adhesive. Repeat for the remaining frame tags. Adhere two frame tags back sides together, using pieces of double-sided super tape; cut to fit. Set the frame tags aside.

3. To create an eye pin, cut a 2" length of 20-gauge wire. Grasp the wire in the jaws of a pair of round-nose pliers near the tip and roll the wire forward to make a loop. Remove the round-nose pliers and use the chain-nose pliers to grab the base of the loop along the longest length of wire. Rotate your hand back, bending the loop at a sharp angle. Remove the pliers and reinsert the round-nose pliers into the loop; rotate the wire forward to make a full circle with a stem that is centered exactly under the circle.

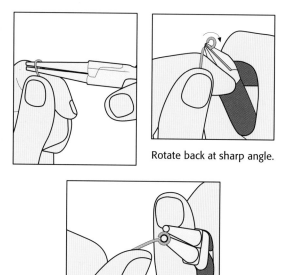

Rotate back at sharp angle.

4. Thread a green seed bead, a 10-mm red bead, and another green seed bead, in that order, onto the remaining end. Trim the wire to a scant ⅜" and make another loop in the same manner. Repeat to make a total of 215 beaded lengths with a wire loop at each end. Follow the same method to add wire to six 14-mm beads and five of the 18-mm beads, substituting bell caps for the green seed beads. Using the same method, also add wire to the green spiral beads. For the remaining 18-mm red bead, thread a bell cap, bead, and then

another bell cap onto the gold head pin and make a loop in the wire at the top.

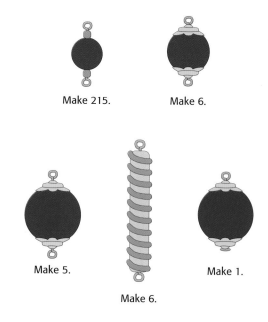

Make 215.   Make 6.

Make 5.   Make 1.

Make 6.

5. Join two red and green bead lengths together to make a bead segment for each of the five beaded drops. Join 23 red and green bead lengths together to make each of five outer swags. Join 18 red and green bead lengths together to make each of five inner swags. To join the beads, hold a bead and grasp half of one eye in the jaws of chain-nose pliers and rotate your hand forward as shown below. Do not pull the eye apart from the side because that will distort the round shape. Slip the end of the open eye onto the wire loop of a second bead length and close the eye. Close the eye in the same manner in which you opened it, rotating it back to a closed position.

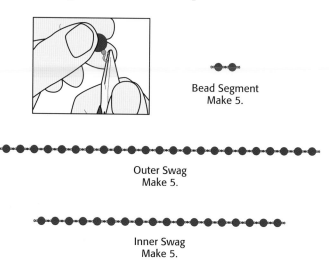

Bead Segment
Make 5.

Outer Swag
Make 5.

Inner Swag
Make 5.

6. To make the beaded drops, join a red and green bead segment, a 14-mm bead, a green spiral bead, and an 18-mm bead in the same manner in which you joined the beaded lengths in step 5. Then open the remaining loop on the 18-mm bead and slip the double-frame tag with photos onto the loop. Then close the loop to make a beaded drop. Repeat to make a total of five beaded drops, one for each arm of the chande-lier. Join the remain-ing 14-mm red bead, green spiral bead, and 18-mm red bead in the same manner to make the beaded drop for the center ring of the chandelier.

Make 1.

Photo

Make 5.

7. To make the support for the beaded swags, cut a 15" length of 18-gauge wire. Wrap the wire twice around a ¼" rod a couple of inches from one end. Twist the ends once to secure them, and then pull the ends out at a 90° angle. Center the double loop on the outside of the chandelier just under the candle holder. Wrap the longer end of the wire around the inside of the chande-lier and back to the outside. Make a cou-ple of wraps around the base of the dou-ble loop and trim the excess from both ends. Repeat at the remain-ing four arms of the chandelier.

Make double loop.

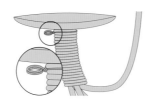

Wrap wire end around inside of chandelier arm, wrap around base of loop, and trim excess.

8. Cut a 15" length of 18-gauge wire and make a double loop as in step 7. Center the double loop under the candle holder on the inside of the chandelier at the point where the chande-lier arms are attached to the candleholder. Wrap the longer end of the wire around the outside of the chandelier and back to the inside. Make a couple of wraps around the base of the double loop and trim the excess wire. Repeat for the remaining four arms of the chandelier.

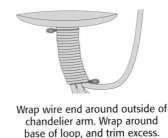

Wrap wire end around outside of chandelier arm. Wrap around base of loop, and trim excess.

9. Measure the distance between the chandelier arms at the center interior of the chandelier where the arms meet. Cut about a 26" length of 18-gauge wire. Make five double loops in the wire spaced the measured distance apart. Wrap the wire with double loops around the upper edge of the interior support of the chan-delier. Join the ends of the wire at one of the double loops by wrapping one end of the wire a couple of times around the base of the last double loop on the other end of the wire. Trim the excess wire.

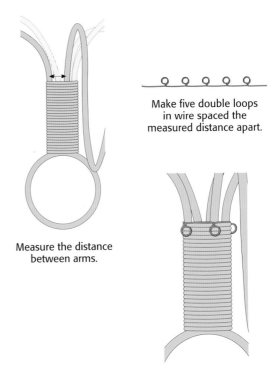

Make five double loops in wire spaced the measured distance apart.

Measure the distance between arms.

Wrap wire around interior support.

10. Wrap 20-gauge wire 25 times around a ¼" rod. Remove the wire from the rod and pull the coil apart until there is some space between the coils. Trim the end flush. Then trim apart the coils to make 25 jump rings, making a flush cut on each end of the wire. Open the jump rings as for loops on eye pins. Join three to each double loop on the outside arms of the chandelier. Join one to each double loop on the inside arms and to each double loop around the center support of the chandelier.

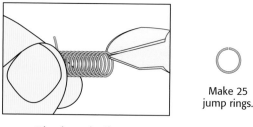

Make 25 jump rings.

Trim rings of coil apart to make jump rings.

11. Join the outer swags to the chandelier by connecting the loops of the end beads to a jump ring at the outside of each chandelier arm. Use the right and left jump rings to join the beaded swags on the right and left sides of the arm. Then join a beaded drop to the center jump ring on the outside arm.

12. Join the inner swags to the chandelier by connecting the end loops of the swags to the jump rings at the inside of each chandelier arm and to the jump rings around the center support of the chandelier.

13. To make the beaded drop at the center, wrap a 20" piece of 18-gauge wire once around the center loop of the chandelier and twist it once to secure it. Place the ¼" rod directly below the center loop and wrap one end of the wire around it. Then make a couple of wraps around the previous twist. Trim the ends and remove the ¼" rod. Join the remaining beaded drop to the wire loop at the center bottom of the chandelier.

DESIGNER'S TIP

For added holiday charm, insert short sprigs of cedar and red artificial berries into the center of the chandelier. Arch the cedar sprigs along the chandelier frame, securing them with short pieces of 20-gauge wire. Also attach short sprigs of cedar to the inside arms of the chandelier using pieces of 20-gauge wire.

STENCILED HOLLY SERVING TRAY

BY JENNIFER FERGUSON

Delight your guests with holiday goodies served upon this charming stenciled tray. It features a traditional holiday motif but is given a whimsical flare with its polka-dot ball feet and shiny red glass handles. Make one for yourself or create one to give as a gift.

Materials

+ Wooden tray, 12" x 14" x 2"
+ 4 wooden ball knobs, 2¼"
+ 2 decorative drawer handles with hardware
+ Gesso
+ Americana Acrylic Paints in the following colors: Buttermilk, Sand, Burgundy Wine, Napa Red, Burnt Umber, Hauser Light Green, and Evergreen
+ Americana Satin Varnish
+ Paint palette
+ 1" flat brush
+ 2" foam brush
+ Stencilled Garden Stencils (see "Sources" on page 96): Gingham (TSG112S), Holly Vine (TSG196); or stencil patterns on pages 60–61.
+ Painter's tape
+ Stencil brushes
+ Paper towels
+ E6000 adhesive
+ Drill and drill bit of correct size to install drawer handles
+ Embossing tool

Note: If you are making your own stencils, you will also need:

+ Access to a photocopy machine
+ Template plastic
+ Pen
+ X-Acto knife
+ Self-healing cutting mat

Stenciling Basics

Loading the brush: Pour a small amount of paint onto your paint palette and dip the brush into the paint. Work the paint into the bristles by rubbing in a circular motion on a clean area of the palette. Hold the brush upright and rub the excess paint onto a folded paper towel, rubbing in a circular motion; then wipe the brush across the paper towel in an X motion to remove the excess paint.

Applying the paint: Hold the brush upright and apply the paint by swirling the brush around in a circular motion into the stencil openings.

Shading: To add more than a single paint color to a given area, creating shading and depth, allow the first layer of paint to dry completely. Then use a new brush to apply the second color.

Instructions

1. Prime the wooden tray and ball knobs with gesso, using the 1"-wide flat brush.

2. Paint the wooden tray with Buttermilk and the ball knobs with Burgundy Wine, using your 1"-wide flat brush. Apply several coats to achieve opaque, even coverage. Allow the paint to dry between coats.

3. To create the stripes on the sides of the tray on both the interior and exterior, start by pouring a small amount of Sand onto your paint palette. Dilute the paint with water. Then use the 1"-wide flat brush to paint the stripes freehand, spacing them approximately 1" apart. These stripes should be soft and whimsical in

appearance rather than precise. This technique works best with a newer brush.

4. Paint the top edge of the tray with Burgundy Wine. A 2" foam brush works best for this edge. Apply several coats, being sure not to use too much pressure.

5. If you are making yur own stencils, photocopy the patterns for the gingham background, the holly vine, and the holly leaf and berry clusters on pages 60–61. Transfer each of the holly designs twice and the gingham design three times onto template plastic with a pen. For the holly vine design, cut out the leaves and vines from one piece of plastic (stencil overlay #1); cut on the marked lines with an X-Acto knife and cutting mat. Cut out the berries only on the remaining piece of plastic (stencil overlay #2). For the holly leaf and berry clusters, cut out the leaves only from one piece of plastic (stencil overlay #1) and the berries only from the other piece of plastic (stencil overlay #2). For the gingham design, cut out all of the pieces labeled 1 on one piece of plastic (stencil overlay #1), all of the pieces labeled 2 on the second piece of plastic (stencil overlay #2), and all of the pieces labeled 3 on the third piece of plastic (stencil overlay #3).

6. Tape gingham background stencil overlay #1 to the inside bottom of the tray and stencil with Sand paint. Refer to "Stenciling Basics" on page 58. Allow to dry. Move and realign stencil as necessary to stencil the entire bottom of the tray. Repeat with gingham background stencil overlays #2 and #3, aligning the stencil openings with the previously stenciled areas, to complete the gingham pattern.

7. Tape the holly vine stencil overlay #1 to one of the exterior sides of the tray. Stencil the holly leaves with Hauser Light Green and shade them on one side with Evergreen. Refer to "Stenciling Basics" on page 58. Stencil the vine with Burnt Umber. Remove and reposition the stencil as necessary. Align the holly vine stencil overlay #2 over the previously stenciled leaves and stencil the holly berries with Napa Red paint.

8. Using holly leaf and berry cluster stencil overlay #1, stencil a pair of holly leaves on top of the gingham design on the inside bottom of the tray with Hauser Light Green and Evergreen in the same manner as for the sides. Align holly leaf and berry cluster stencil overlay #2 over the stenciled leaves and stencil a cluster of berries next to the pair of leaves with Napa Red. Repeat the process to stencil similar groupings of leaves and berries over the entire interior bottom of the tray, placing the groupings randomly, with about 3" between groupings. Repeat to stencil leaf and berry groupings in the interior sides of the tray, placing three groupings along each side.

9. Using an embossing tool, apply dots to the wooden ball knobs with Sand paint.

10. Allow all paint to dry for several days. Protect the painted design by applying at least three coats of varnish to the tray and wooden ball knobs, allowing the varnish to dry thoroughly between coats.

11. Attach the wooden ball knobs to the base of the tray using the E6000 adhesive.

12. Install decorative drawer handles, centered along the sides, on the exterior of the tray.

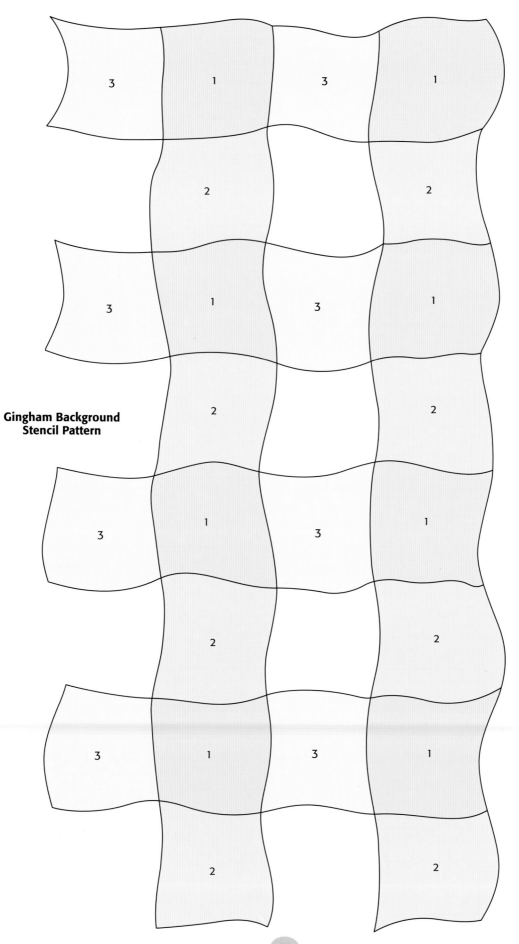

**Gingham Background
Stencil Pattern**

Holly Vine Stencil Pattern

Holly Leaf and Berry Cluster
Stencil Pattern

AROUND THE HOUSE

EMBROIDERED CHRISTMAS HAND TOWELS

BY LINDA WYSZYNSKI

Add embroidered tree and wreath motifs to ready-made linen guest towels to transform them into festive accents for the holidays. These towels are created using three simple stitches and are further accented with red seed beads.

Materials

- 2 white linen hand towels with hemstitched borders
- 6-strand embroidery floss (DMC) in the following colors:
  - Christmas Red Medium No. 304
  - Christmas Green Light No. 701
  - Kelly Green No. 702
- Frosted red seed beads (Mill Hill No. 62013)
- Silver marking pencil (Dritz)
- Ruler
- Tracing paper
- ¼"-wide quilter's tape (Wrights)
- Embroidery and beading needles
- White and red sewing thread
- Black fine-line waterproof pen
- Light box or sunlit window

Transferring Patterns

Trace the tree and wreath patterns on page 67 onto tracing paper, using a black pen. Place each pattern face up on the back of a towel. Center each design across the width of the towel, about 1" above the hemstitched border. Tape the patterns in place with quilter's tape. Position the towel, pattern side down, over a sunlit window or light box. Use the silver marking pencil to trace the designs onto the towels. Do not trace the individual pine needles or berries as the lines could show. You will stitch them on randomly after the other stitching is complete. Use the ruler when tracing the tree branches to help keep the lines straight. Be sure to use a sharp pencil.

DESIGNER'S TIPS

- Use the embroidery needle to work the embroidery stitches and the beading needle to attach the beads.

- Use two strands of floss for the embroidery stitches. When working on a linen towel, the floss may show through from the back side depending on the thread count of the linen. If the thread does show through, it will be necessary to begin and end your stitching where the design lines begin and end.

- To begin, place a very small knot in the end of the floss. To end, run your floss ends under previously placed stitches and trim thread tails as necessary.

- Rinse the colored thread before you begin stitching so that the colors will not bleed when you wash the towel. Hold the thread under cold water until the water is clear. Gently blot it on a paper towel. If the color bleeds onto the paper towel, repeat the process. Allow the thread to completely dry before stitching.

Stitching Instructions (Wreath)

Refer to the stitching diagrams on page 67 for embroidery stitches. Bring your needle up from the back of the fabric at A, down at B, and up at C and continue in this manner until the stitching is complete.

1. Using the red floss, stitch the bow on the wreath, using a satin stitch. Work the center of the bow so that the stitches run horizontally. Work the satin stitches parallel to each other, being sure the threads completely cover the white area within the design lines and lie smoothly. Work the loops of the bow with the stitches placed at a slight angle. Compensate around the outer curves by filling in the gaps with one or more short stitches as shown in the compensating satin stitch diagram on page 67.

2. Using the Christmas Green Light floss, stem stitch the main branches of the wreath. Keep the thread on the lower side of the needle while working the stitches.

3. Using the Kelly Green floss, straight stitch the needles onto the branches. Use the pattern on page 67 as a guide for placement.

4. Use the white sewing thread to randomly stitch the beads to the wreath. Use the pattern on page 67 as a guide for placement. To be sure the beads are secure, stitch through each bead twice. When traveling from bead to bead, run your thread under the stitches on the back.

Stitching Instructions (Tree)

Refer to the stitching diagrams on page 67 for embroidery stitches. Bring your needle up from the back of the fabric at A, down at B, up at C, and continue in this manner until the stitching is complete.

1. Using the Christmas Green Light floss, stem stitch the main branches of the tree. Keep the thread on the lower side of the needle while working the stitches.

2. Using the Kelly Green floss, straight stitch the needles onto the branches. Use the pattern on page 67 as a guide for placement.

3. Using the Christmas Green Light floss and the satin stitch, fill in the tree holder. Stem stitch a row around the outside of the holder.

4. Use the white sewing thread to randomly stitch the beads to the tree. Use the pattern on page 67 as a guide for placement. To be sure the beads are secure, stitch through each bead twice. When traveling from bead to bead, run your thread under the stitches on the back. Use the red sewing thread to attach four beads to the center of the tree holder as shown in the pattern.

Satin Stitch   Compensating Satin Stitch   Stem Stitch   Straight Stitch

Embroidery Stitches

Wreath   Tree

Embroidery Patterns

BEADED CANDLE WREATH

BY CHRISTINE FALK

Create this stunning candle wreath with a couple of simple beading techniques. Faceted ruby beads are used to make berry clusters on wire stems, and matching seed beads are used to create the beaded leaves. The wire stems of the beaded clusters and leaves are twisted together to make a wreath, and the wreath base is covered with floral tape to conceal the joined ends.

Materials

- 50 ruby-red fire-polished round beads, 10 mm
- 90 ruby-red fire-polished round beads, 8 mm
- 110 ruby-red fire-polished round beads, 6 mm
- 1 hank of size 10 garnet seed beads
- 28-gauge tinned copper spool wire
- 26-gauge tinned copper spool wire
- Brown floral tape
- 3 pillar candles
- Shallow dish
- Needle-nose pliers
- Wire cutters
- 8"-diameter glass cake plate or candle holder

DESIGNER'S TIP

To keep the base of the wreath as inconspicuous as possible, choose a floral tape that blends with the color of your beads. It is available in light and dark green, plus brown and white. When assembling the wreath, snip a few of the wires after about every four branches and wrap the floral tape tightly around the wires so that the taped part of the wreath does not get too thick.

Instructions for Beaded Leaves

1. Pour the seed beads into a shallow dish. Thread approximately 12" of seed beads onto a spool of 28-gauge wire. Make a small loop in the end of the wire and twist it to prevent the beads from slipping off the end (this is the center wire). Slide nine beads toward the loop (these become the center row of the leaf). About 6" below the looped end, create a larger loop using 8" of wire and twist the wire several times. This loop will become the stem. Make sure the nine beads stay between the small and large loops.

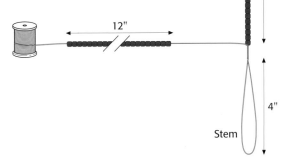

2. Hold the large loop in one hand and with your other hand slide enough beads down to wrap around the left side of the original nine center beads, but extend one bead beyond the top of the nine center beads. Let the top bead rest above the nine beads on the center wire and

wrap the spool wire at a 45° angle across the front side of the center wire, around the back, and back around to the front.

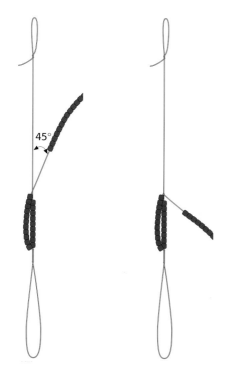

3. Slide enough beads down to wrap around the right side of the original nine center beads. Wrap the wire once around the twisted wire above the large loop. This completes one row around the leaf center. Continue to add rows of beads around the center beads, making sure each row is slightly longer than the previous row to create the tip of the leaf. Maintain the 45° angle at the tip of the leaf every time you wrap wire. As rows are added, the bead rows should rest against each other. The leaf is complete when four rows have been added to each side of the center row.

4. To finish the leaf, wrap bare spool wire tightly twice around the wire at the base of the leaf. Trim with wire cutters. Bend the top wire to the back of the leaf and trim to about ¼". Use your fingers to press the trimmed end against the beads. Shape the leaf carefully, emphasizing the point and verifying that the rows are lined up well. Too much movement can cause the wire to break, so work gently.

Instructions for Wreath

1. To start the wreath, create "branches" of beads using an assortment of 6-mm, 8-mm, and 10-mm fire-polished beads. Branches can be made using three, four, or five beads per branch. To create a branch, thread one bead onto a 20" length of 26-gauge or 28-gauge wire (use 26-gauge for larger beads, 28-gauge for smaller beads). Push a bead to the center of the wire. Pinch the wire under the bead and twist the bead until the twisted part of the wire reaches ¾" to 1½" in length. Add another bead to one end of the wire. Slide the bead up to about 1" to 2" from the twisted part of the wire. Pinch the wire under the bead and begin twisting the bead until the twisted part of the wire reaches ¾" to 1½" in length or meets the bottom of the first twisted wire. Pinch two twisted wires at their base and begin twisting for about ¼" to ½" in length. Add a third bead to one end of the wire. Slide it up to about 1" to 2" below the twisted wire and pinch the wire under the bead. Begin twisting the third bead until the twisted part of the wire reaches ¾" to 1½" in length or reaches the other twisted wires. Stop here or add one or two more beads in the same manner. Twist the wire

ends together for about 1". The beaded cluster will begin to resemble a tree branch. Create approximately 60 branches.

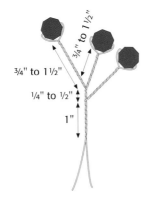

2. To assemble the wreath, bunch two or three branches and begin taping them together with floral tape just under the twisted part of the wires. Pull the tape to release the wax. Wrap the wires at an angle. Wrap them tightly so that the floral tape does not become too thick. Continue to add branches one or two at a time, interspersing beaded leaves at approximately 2" intervals.

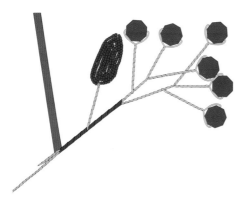

After every four branches or so, snip a few of the wires so that the taped part of the wreath does not get too thick. Build the wreath until it reaches about 22" in length. Connect the ends with floral tape, completing the circle. Place the wreath around the three pillar candles along the edge of a cake plate or candle holder. Bend the wires to fill in gaps and create a pleasing arrangement.

BOXWOOD WREATH
WITH BEADED FRUIT

BY DAWN ANDERSON

You can hang this boxwood wreath inside or hang it outside in a protected area. The fresh greens will stay fresh longer outside. If the wreath is hung indoors, the greens will begin to dry after about a week but will retain their green color for several months.

Materials

+ 4 to 5 bunches of fresh boxwood
+ 8 pieces of assorted beaded fruit on wire stems (pomegranates, apples, and pears)
+ 1 bunch of seeded eucalyptus or blackberry privet
+ 2 to 3 artificial berry stems
+ Kraft paper
+ 20" round wreath form
+ 22-gauge paddle wire
+ 18-gauge 18" florist wire stems
+ Pruning shears
+ Wire cutters

Instructions

1. Cover your work surface with kraft paper. Using pruning shears, clip boxwood branches into 6" to 8" sprigs. Hold three to four sprigs together and bind them with a 12" length of paddle wire. Repeat to make about 30 bundles.

2. Hold one bundle against the outer edge of the wreath form and bind it in place with an 18" length of wire.

Position a second bundle on top of the first bundle, with the ends about 2" away from the ends of the first bundle and the wire binding concealed. Bind it in place. Continue in this manner around the entire outer wire of the wreath form. Then bind the bundles around the middle wires of the wreath form in the same manner, tilting them inward so that they cover the inner wire as well. Cut sprigs of seeded eucalyptus or blackberry privet and wire them to the wreath base, centered across the width of the wreath.

3. Insert the fruit around the wreath, spacing it evenly and centering it across the width. Carefully lift the wreath and twist the fruit stems around the wire wreath frame to secure them in place.

4. Cut apart the berry stems using wire cutters to make eight clusters. Fold one stem of florist wire in half and insert it between two arms of the berry cluster. Wrap the wires around the front and then the back of the berry stem in a crisscross manner. Insert the wire ends of the berry cluster into the wreath between two pieces of fruit. Lift the wreath and wrap the wire ends around the wire wreath frame to secure. Repeat with the remaining berry clusters.

5. Fold a piece of 18-gauge wire in half and twist the ends together about 3" from the fold to make a loop for hanging the wreath. Wrap the ends of the wire securely around the wire wreath form on the back side.

MOSAIC SNOWFLAKE LUMINARY

BY JILL MacKAY

This snowflake luminary will charm and entrance you as it twinkles with candlelight. It will add light and beauty to your holiday table setting and provide flickering warmth through your winter months.

Materials

+ 1 glass luminary, 13" tall x 4¾" in diameter
+ 12" x 12" piece of textured clear glass
+ 12" x 12" piece of frosted white stained glass
+ 12" x 12" piece of translucent aqua stained glass
+ 3-ounce tube of clear silicone glue
+ 2 pounds of white sanded grout
+ 1 ounce of Folk Art acrylic color in Phthalo Blue (Plaid)
+ Access to a photocopy machine
+ Glass cleaner
+ Paper towels
+ Masking tape, 1" wide
+ Paper plates
+ Old towel
+ Craft sticks
+ Plastic drop cloth
+ 2 plastic buckets or containers
+ Dust mask
+ Rubber gloves
+ Sponge
+ Soft polishing cloth (not terry cloth)
+ Razor blade
+ Breaking pliers
+ Gallery glasses or safety glasses (Plaid)
+ Hand-held glass cutter
+ Mosaic glass cutters (Plaid)

DESIGNER'S TIPS

+ You will not use all of the glass listed in the materials list. I have specified 12" x 12" sheets because this is a standard size in which stained glass is sold. If you work in stained glass, you may not have to purchase any additional glass. Use your scrap, especially the white. You will use the least of this color.

+ Protect your eyes by always wearing safety goggles when cutting glass.

+ When gluing the aqua blue glass in place to fill the swirl shapes, have the pieces of glass follow the directional arrows placed on the pattern to create movement and add strength to the design.

+ Leave approximately ¼" of space at the top lip of the luminary. Below this space keep the edge of the glass very straight and even to give a clean, professional look to the piece.

+ If you find that your pieces are slipping or sliding when you glue them onto the luminary, lay the luminary on its side on an old cushion or towel to work on it.

+ When you score or cut the glass, you do not need to use a ruler. Work freehand and "eyeball" the cuts. Cut the white and the aqua stained glass loosely into rectangles. Cut the clear glass into shards of different shapes and sizes. This creates contrast between the stained and clear glass, stimulating more visual interest in the overall effect.

Instructions

1. Photocopy or trace the patterns on pages 77–78. Clean the luminary with glass cleaner and paper towels. Roll the snowflake pattern (face out) and place it inside the luminary. Trim the paper down and tape it in place if necessary.

2. Put on safety glasses. Score three $3/16$" x 12" strips of white glass. Use the breaking pliers to snap off each of the 12"-long glass strips. Hold each strip over a paper plate and use the mosaic cutters to nip the strips into rectangles from $1/4$" to $3/8$" in length.

3. Follow the pattern and glue the white pieces of glass onto the luminary to create the snowflake. Use a craft stick to spread the glue onto the surface of the luminary, or if the glue has a nozzle you can spread it with the tip. Spread a couple of inches of glue at a time. Then place the glass pieces in the glue. Working in sections like this allows you to complete the mosaic work in a single area before the glue dries.

4. Remove the snowflake pattern and insert the first swirl pattern into the luminary on the right of the snowflake so that the bottom tip is just to the right of the center bottom arm of the snowflake (see photograph). Tape in place. Use the glass cutter to score eight $3/16$" x 12" strips of aqua stained glass. Using the breaking pliers, snap off each of the 12" strips. Then, carefully holding each strip over a paper plate, nip it into rectangles ranging from $1/4$" to $1/2$" in length, using the mosaic cutters. As you proceed, use the mosaic cutters to cut and nip pieces of glass to reshape them when necessary. Glue the pieces to the luminary following the swirl design.

5. Remove the first swirl pattern and insert the second swirl pattern into the luminary on the left of the snowflake so that the top tip is just to the left of the center top arm of the snowflake. Position the swirl to fill the remaining space around the luminary. Repeat the mosaic process for the second swirl in the same manner as the first. Use the mosaic cutters to nip and shape the remaining pieces of aqua glass to fit inside the inner circles and center of the snowflake, gluing each piece in place as you work.

6. Score several 12"-long strips of the clear glass, $3/8$" to $1/2$" wide, with the glass cutter (score more as you go if needed). Using the breaking pliers, snap off each of the 12"-long strips. Holding the strips carefully over a paper plate, use the mosaic cutters to nip the strips into shards of different shapes and sizes. Gluing a small section at a time, fill in the background by cutting and nipping pieces to fit with the mosaic cutters. Turn the luminary over if necessary while filling in the bottom portion of the body.

7. Using the glass cutter, score three $3/16$" x 12"-strips of aqua glass. Snap off each of the 12"-long strips using the breaking pliers. Carefully hold each strip over a paper plate and use the mosaic cutters to nip the strips into small shards. Shape and nip these shards so that they are small enough to lie flat on the surface. If you can rock a shard back and forth when you are pressing it against the surface, the shard is too large. Glue glass shards to the surface of the foot, leaving $1/4$" of space on the outside edge. Let the piece dry overnight.

8. Using the razor blade, carefully remove any dried glue from the surface of the glass. Cover your work surface with the drop cloth in preparation for grouting. Fill one bucket with water. Put on a dust mask and rubber gloves and pour approximately $1\frac{1}{4}$ pounds of grout into the other bucket. Follow the manufacturer's instructions and mix the grout by adding the water slowly. While the mix is still somewhat dry, add approximately 2 tablespoons of the blue acrylic paint; mix thoroughly. The grout should be the consistency of thick oatmeal.

9. Apply the grout carefully over the entire surface of the luminary's main body. With your gloved fingertips, push the grout down into spaces and crevices. Spread it in many different directions. Use your fingertips to place grout along the top edge, creating a ¼"-thick grout line all the way around the top. Smooth this grout line with your fingertips to get an even, straight line at the top edge. Spread the grout over the surface of the mosaic work on the foot of the luminary, making sure to have grout on the top and lower edges. Smooth these edges with your fingertip. Let the grout set for 10 to 15 minutes. Dampen a sponge by dipping it in water and wringing out the excess. Sponge away excess grout, being careful not to remove too much. You may need to go back and fix or touch up the edges if small amounts of grout were dislodged during sponging. Let the piece dry another 15 to 20 minutes and then polish it with a clean soft cloth.

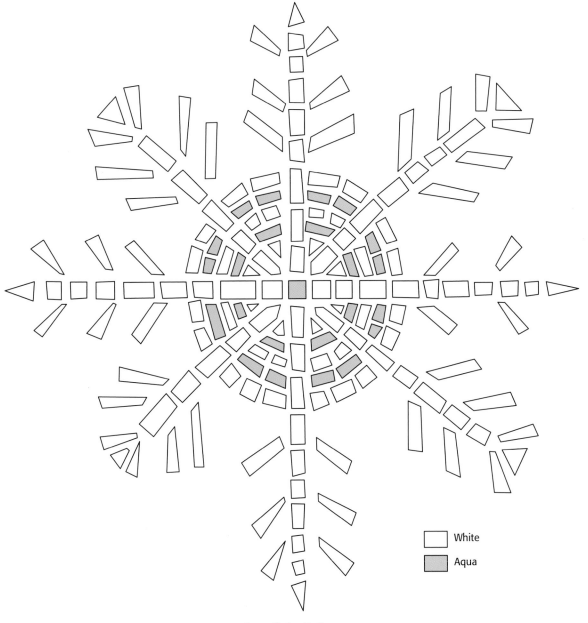

White

Aqua

Snowflake Pattern

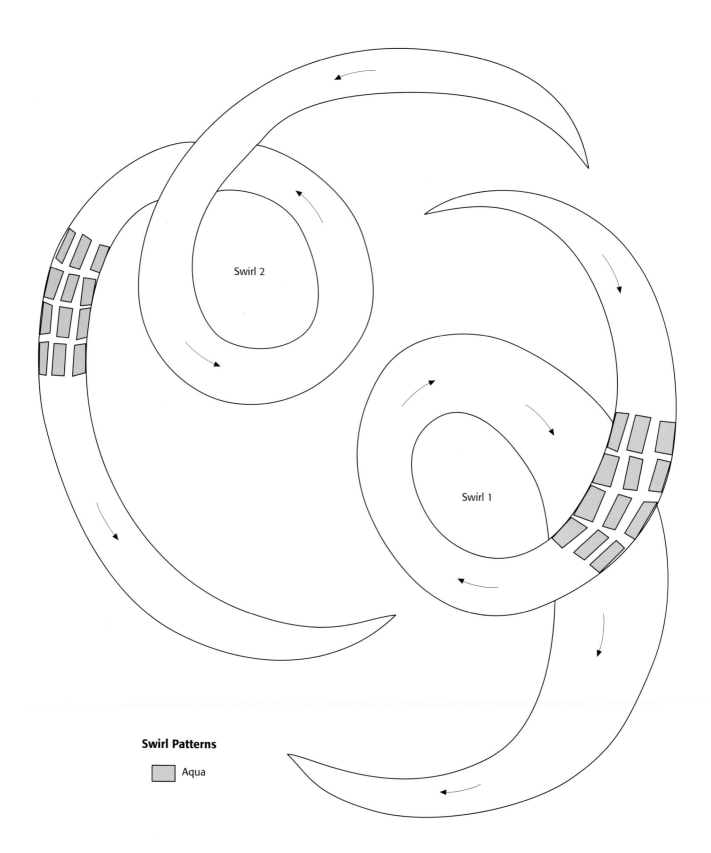

Swirl Patterns

Aqua

PAINTED JOY CANVASES

BY SARALYN EWALD, Creative Coordinator, Archiver's: The Photo Memory Store

Paint plain white artist's canvases with a simple greeting to add holiday cheer to your home. Choose shades of green and teal to create the "Joy" canvases shown here, or you may want to try a traditional red and green color scheme with the word "Noel." You don't need to be a skilled painter to achieve success with this simple project.

Materials

+ Three 6" x 6" canvases (Blick Art Materials)
+ Plaid Folk Art Acrylic Paint in the following colors: Icy White, Teal, Hunter Green, Hauser Green Medium, and Mint Green
+ Newsprint
+ 5" x 5" square of heavy paper or cardboard
+ Pencil
+ Computer and printer
+ 3 sheets of heavy cardstock (any color)
+ Paper towels
+ Clean white eraser
+ Loew-Cornell brushes:
  • Series 7300 Shader sizes #6 and #14
  • Series 7500 Filbert size #10/0
+ Sharp, pointed scissors

DESIGNER'S TIPS

+ Apply as many coats of paint as needed for desired coverage.

+ Allow paint to dry between coats. The paint will dry slightly darker than it appears when wet.

+ The letters for these canvases were created on a computer. If you do not have access to a computer, you can easily substitute alphabet stencils.

Instructions

1. Protect your work surface with newsprint. Place the canvases over the newsprint. Paint the front surface of each canvas with Icy White paint, using the #14 shader brush.

2. Using the photo on page 79 as a guide for placement, place the 5" x 5" square of paper or cardboard off-center onto the front of one canvas, keeping the edges parallel to the edges of the canvas. Trace around the square, using a pencil. Repeat on the remaining two canvases, positioning the square slightly differently on each canvas.

3. Using a desktop publishing program, select the font and size of the letters to fit within a 5" x 5" box. Print the letters onto heavy cardstock.

4. Using sharp, pointed scissors, carefully cut out each letter from the cardstock. Position a letter inside each traced box, slightly overlapping the box on at least one edge. Lightly trace each letter with a pencil.

5. Paint inside the traced boxes, around the letters, using a #10/0 filbert to outline the area and the #6 shader to fill in. Use Teal paint to paint around the *J*, Hunter Green to paint around the *O*, and Hauser Green Medium to paint around the *Y*. One coat of paint should be enough. Allow it to dry.

6. Prepare a slightly lighter color tint to paint around each letter, over the previously painted area, by mixing some of the main paint color (Teal for the *J*) with a small amount of Icy White. Use a dry brush (#6 shader) to apply light, streaky layers over the painted boxes to give the color some visual texture. Be careful to avoid painting inside the letter. If too much paint is applied, use a paper towel to wipe the excess paint while it is still wet. Allow the paint to dry.

7. Gently erase any visible pencil lines with a clean, white eraser.

8. Paint the side edges of the canvases with Mint Green, using the #6 shader brush, painting one side at a time. Be careful not to have too much paint on your brush as you paint around the edges or the paint may run onto the front of the canvas.

DESIGNER'S TIP

Use this versatile project any time of the year, using the same technique to paint a different message. Display "EAT" in your kitchen, "CREATE" in your studio, or hang children's names on their bedroom walls.

BEADED STOCKING

BY DAWN ANDERSON

This holiday stocking, made in traditional Christmas red and green, is given a whimsical look with a pointed toe. The stocking cuff is richly finished with velvet ribbon edged with rows of bugle beads. Beaded fringe hangs from the lower edge of the cuff and a beaded drop dangles from the tip of the toe.

Materials

- ¾ yard of 45"-wide red silk dupioni
- ¼ yard of 45"-wide green silk dupioni
- ⅝ yard of red velvet ribbon, 15 mm (Mokuba)
- ¾ yard of lining
- ⅝ yard of 20"-wide fusible knit interfacing
- ⅝ yard of 45"-wide flannel
- Thread to match fabrics
- Hand-sewing needle
- Pins
- ½"-wide fusible tape (Steam-A-Seam 2)
- Masking tape
- Pen
- 1 hank of green bugle beads, 2 mm x 4.5 mm
- 1 hank of red silver-lined size 11 seed beads
- 90 green diamond-shaped beads, size 5 mm x 7 mm
- 1 ruby pressed-glass bead, size 10
- 1 jewelry head pin from 20-gauge wire
- Access to a photocopy machine
- Clear grid ruler
- Iron and ironing board
- Pliers: round-nose and chain-nose
- Sewing shears
- Sewing machine

Instructions

1. Cut two stocking pieces each from red silk dupioni, interfacing, and flannel. Cut two stocking lining pieces, trimming the toe as indicated on the pattern. For the cuff, cut two 7" x 17½" rectangles each from green silk and interfacing.

2. Fuse the interfacing pieces to the wrong sides of the red stocking pieces and green cuff pieces, following the manufacturer's directions. Pin the flannel stocking pieces to the wrong sides of the red stocking pieces and baste ⅜" from all edges.

3. Pin the stocking pieces right sides together. Stitch ½" from the curved edges. Trim seam allowances to a scant ¼"; notch convex curves and clip concave curves. Pin the lining pieces right sides together. Stitch the curved edge, increasing the seam allowance to ¾" around the foot and leaving a 4" opening in the back seam. Trim the seam allowances to ¼". Press the front and back seams open on both the stocking and lining.

Pin the cuff pieces right sides together on one long edge. Stitch ½" from the long edge. Trim the seam and press open.

4. Cut a 17½" length each of velvet ribbon and fusible tape. Position the adhesive side of the tape onto the wrong side of the ribbon. Remove backing paper from the tape and position the ribbon on the stocking cuff 1⅛" above the seam line. Press in place with an iron.

5. Thread a beading needle with a 20" length of beading thread. Stitch bugle beads along the edge of the ribbon. Position the first row on the edge of the ribbon, starting 1" from one short end of the cuff. Bring the needle up at 1, go through one bead, insert the needle down at 2, and then come back up at 1. Insert the needle through the same bead again and then through a second bead and down into the fabric at 3. Bring the needle back up at 2 and through the last bead. Continue in the same manner across the cuff until you reach 1" from the opposite end (knotting thread on the back side after every 1" of beading). Stitch a total of two rows of bugle beads on each side of the ribbon.

DESIGNER'S TIP

Bugle beads vary slightly in length. When stitching the second row of beads on each side of the ribbon, take care with each stitch to select a bead that matches the length of the bead used in the previous row. This keeps the ends of the beads in both rows aligned for a neat finish.

6. Cut a piece of masking tape the length of the cuff and make marks on one edge ⅜" apart. Place tape on the cuff with the marked edge of the tape along the seam line. Thread the beading needle with a 24" length of beading thread. Insert the needle along the cuff seam line, to one side of seam allowances from the back side, about 1" from one short end of the cuff. Thread as follows: seed bead, bugle bead, seed bead, bugle bead, seed bead, bugle bead, seed

bead, diamond bead, and a final seed bead onto the needle and slide up to cuff seam line. Thread the needle back through all beads except the final seed bead added and insert the needle into the back side of the cuff to make a short length of fringe. Take a stitch ⅜" from the first length of fringe, using markings on the tape as a guide. Thread as follows: seed bead, bugle bead, seed bead, bugle bead, seed bead, diamond bead, seed bead, bugle bead, seed bead, diamond bead, and a final seed bead onto the beading needle and slide up to the cuff seam line. Thread the needle through all but the final seed bead to make a long length of fringe. Insert the needle to the back side of the cuff at the seam line and take a stitch ⅜" away. Continue stitching the fringe along the remainder of the cuff seam line, alternating between short and long lengths. Stop about 1" from the opposite end of the cuff.

7. Pin the short edges of the cuff right sides together, and stitch ½" from the edges. Trim the seam allowance to ¼" and press the seam open. Turn the cuff right side out, fold it along the seam line, and baste the raw edges together. Finish filling in beaded edging on the sides of the ribbon and beaded fringe along lower edges of the cuff at the back seam.

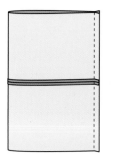

8. Pin the cuff to the upper edge of the stocking, matching the back seams. Fold a 7" length of ribbon in half crosswise and pin its ends, raw edges matching, over the cuff seam. Baste ⅜" from the raw edges all around. Slip the stocking inside the lining, right sides together, and pin the top edges together. Machine stitch ½" from the raw edges, trapping the cuff and ribbon hanger in the seam. Pull the stocking through the opening in the lining and turn the lining right side out.

Slip the stocking inside the lining, right sides together.

9. Slipstitch the lining opening closed and push the lining down inside the stocking. Roll the cuff ⅜" to the inside and lightly press the upper edge.

10. Thread a red bead onto a head pin. Trim the head pin to a scant ⅜" above the bead. Grasp the end of the wire in the jaws of the round-nose pliers near the tip and roll forward to make a loop. Remove the round-nose pliers and with the chain-nose pliers grab the base of the loop along the longest length of wire. Rotate your hand back, bending the loop at a sharp angle. Remove the chain-nose pliers and reinsert the round-nose pliers into the loop as far as they will go. Rotate forward to make a complete circle with a stem that is centered exactly under the circle.

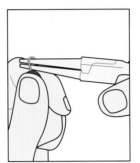 

Rotate back at sharp angle.

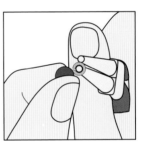

11. Stitch the loop at the end of the bead to the toe of the stocking.

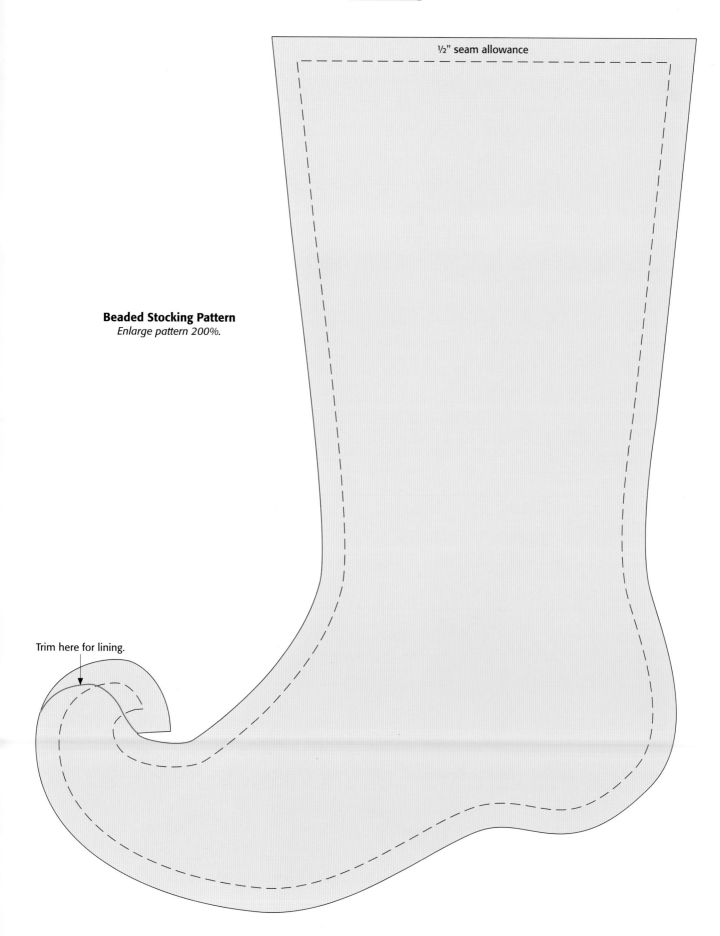

½" seam allowance

Beaded Stocking Pattern
Enlarge pattern 200%.

Trim here for lining.

VICTORIAN FAVOR CUPS

BY GENEVIEVE A. STERBENZ

Use silk shantung, trims, and ribbons to transform simple paper cones into beautiful Christmas decorations, perfect for the tree or as favors for your holiday guests. Accenting the cones with decorative trims and ribbons is what makes these ornaments so much fun to create. And because you can use a glue gun to add these details, you can quickly and easily make enough to dress your entire Christmas tree.

Materials

- Lightweight Bristol board
- 12" squares of silk shantung (solid green, red ⅛" check and green 1/16" check)
- 12" squares of coordinating gift wrap or paper
- Red and green eyelets, ¼" wide (2 per favor cup) and eyelet pliers
- Kraft paper
- Newspaper
- Cardboard
- Spray adhesive
- Pencil
- Clothespins
- Transparent glue stick
- Glue gun and glue sticks
- Clear grid ruler
- Hole punch
- Scissors
- Self-healing cutting mat
- Utility knife
- ¼" hole punch

Trims for Solid Green Favor Cup

- 1½ yards of red and green rose and leaf trim, ⅝" wide
- ½ yard of red braided trim, 5/16" wide
- 1¼ yards of green cording, ⅛" diameter
- ½ yard of green grosgrain ribbon, ¼" wide
- ¾ yard of red grosgrain ribbon, ¼" wide

Trims for Red Checked Favor Cup

- ½ yard of pale green ¼"-loop fringe
- ½ yard of moss green cording, ⅛" diameter
- 2¼ yards of green cording, ⅛" diameter
- ½ yard of red braided trim, 5/16" wide
- 6 red ribbon roses, ½" diameter
- ⅞ yard of red cording, ⅛" diameter
- ½ yard of red grosgrain ribbon, ¼" wide
- ¾ yard of green grosgrain ribbon, ¼" wide

Trims for Green Checked Favor Cup

- ½ yard of pale green ¼"-loop fringe
- 1¼ yards of moss green cording, ⅛" diameter
- ½ yard of red braided trim, ⅜" wide
- 15 red ribbon roses, ¾" wide
- ½ yard of green grosgrain ribbon, ¼" wide
- ¾ yard of red grosgrain ribbon, ¼" wide

DESIGNER'S TIP

All ribbons and trims should be applied with a glue gun. If you are using a very fine trim and feel that the glue gun will apply too much glue, switch to fabric glue that can be better controlled with a toothpick. Use clothespins to hold materials in place until they dry. When applying the ribbons and trims, always begin and end at the back seam of the cone.

Instructions

1. Photocopy or trace the pattern on page 91 twice. Note that you will need to enlarge the pattern 125%. Set one pattern aside. Cover a clean, flat work surface with kraft paper and a second work surface with newspaper. Place the cardboard on the kraft paper and the pattern, wrong side up, on the newspaper. Apply a light coat of spray adhesive to the pattern. Transfer the pattern, turning it to its right side, to the cardboard and laminate the two together, smoothing out any wrinkles or bumps. Place the mounted pattern on a self-healing mat and cut around the outside solid straight lines using a ruler and a utility knife. Use scissors to cut along the curved edge.

2. Place the Bristol board on a clean work surface. Place the mounted pattern from step 1 on the Bristol board and trace around the outline using a pencil. Also create two tick marks, one at the top and one at the bottom, to indicate where the fold line will be. Lift off the pattern and line up the tick marks along a ruler. Draw the fold line with light pencil marks. Then place the Bristol board on a self-healing mat and cut along the straight lines using a straightedge and a utility knife. Use scissors to cut along the curved line. Using the pattern as a guide, trace, mark, and cut a piece of Bristol board for each favor cup. Lay the ruler along the fold line and hold it in place while you bring up the short side. Remove the ruler and make a firm crease along the fold line. Then bring the straight sides together, bending the Bristol board to shape the cone. Do not glue the ends together. Set the cone aside.

3. Place the mounted pattern on the wrong side of the fabric. If the fabric is solid, simply make a rough cut around the pattern, leaving 1" on all sides. If the fabric has a design, set the pattern on the fabric so that the stripes, checks, or other design will appear the way you want it. Then make the rough cut, leaving 1" extra on all sides.

4. Using the cardboard pattern again, follow the directions in step 3 to trace the pattern onto the wrong side of the gift wrap or paper and cut it out. Turn it to the right side, crease along the fold line, and set aside. You will need one liner paper for each favor cup.

5. Lay the fabric, wrong side up, on clean newspaper. Apply a light coat of spray adhesive. Transfer the fabric in the same position to a clean work surface. Place the left short edge of the cone about ½" to ¾" from the left edge of the fabric while holding the right edge up away from the fabric. Press down on the left edge of the Bristol board to adhere it to the fabric. Then, with the same hand, lift up the left edge while smoothing and rolling the cone onto the fabric with the other hand. Laminating the fabric this way will help achieve a smooth application. Laminating a flat pattern to the fabric and then bending it into the cone shape will leave bubbles and creases that cannot be smoothed out. Cut away the excess corner fabric and notch the fabric around the arc. Fold and press the fabric over the edges and onto the inside of the cone.

6. Cut out the extra unmounted pattern. Use a hole punch to make holes where indicated and lay the pattern on the inside of the fabric-laminated Bristol board, lining up the edges. Secure the pattern in place using clothespins. Use a pencil to mark the eyelet holes on the Bristol board. Remove the clothespins and the pattern, and punch holes through the Bristol board and the fabric.

7. Roll the cone so that the ends meet. Tuck the folded flap to the inside. Make sure there is a point at the bottom. Hold the shape in place using a clothespin at the top. Starting at the bottom, run a thin line of glue along the flap to the midpoint and adhere in place. Remove the clothespin and continue applying glue to the remainder of the inside inside flap and secure in place. Place the liner paper right side up. Bring the short edges together and place the folded flap on the outside of the cone. Run dabs of glue along the flap using a transparent glue stick, and press to secure the edges in place. Use the glue stick again to apply a ½"-wide glue strip around the top outer edge of the liner. Lining up the seams, slip the liner into the cone. Press along the top edge to secure the liner to the cone. Line up the hole punch with the previously made holes and punch holes through the liner paper.

8. Slip an eyelet into one hole from the outside. Use the pliers to secure the eyelet in place. Repeat for the opposite hole.

9. **Solid green favor cup:** Measure and cut a 52" length of rose and leaf trim. Beginning at the front bottom point, apply glue to the rose and press to adhere. Wind the trim around the cone in rows, applying glue to the roses only. Glue only a few at a time. Space rows about ¾" apart. Continue wrapping and gluing the trim around the cone until the trim reaches the top edge. Trim away the excess. Measure and cut a 13" length of red braided trim, a 13" length of green grosgrain ribbon, and three 13" lengths of green cording. Starting at the back seam, glue the red braided trim along the top outside edge. This trim will cover some of the rose and leaf trim. Trim the ends flush at the back seam. Glue one length of the green cording to the top edge of the cone; trim the ends flush at the back seam. To finish the inside, glue one length of green cording on the top inside lip of the cone; trim the ends flush at the back seam. Below that, glue the length of green grosgrain ribbon. Below the ribbon, glue the last length of green cording. To create the ribbon handle, measure and cut one 17" and two 4" lengths of red grosgrain ribbon. Thread one end of the 17" length from the inside through the eyelet and tie a double knot. Make sure the ribbon is not twisted, and thread the opposite end from the inside of the cone through the eyelet. Tie a double knot. From the outside of the cone, pull the ribbon at one side to create some slack. Use one of the 4" lengths to tie a bow over the knot in the end of the ribbon. Trim the ends of the bow even and snip away any extra ribbon that extends down below the original knot. Repeat on the opposite side. Pull the ribbon handle from the center to eliminate the slack, bringing the bows up against the eyelets. Place a dab of glue behind the bow and press to adhere to the side of the favor cup. Repeat on the opposite side.

Red checked favor cup: Measure and cut 13" lengths of the following: loop fringe, moss green cording, and red braided trim. Leave the remaining length of the green cording intact. Glue the loop fringe, which is anchored to a plain cotton header, to the inside top lip of the cone. Glue the 13" length of the green cording right below the bottom edge of the loop fringe on the outside of the cone. Below that, glue the length of red braided trim. To create the draped green cording, begin at the back seam and glue the end only below the red trim. Leave some slack in the cording, roughly ¾" from the top edge of the cone. Adhere the cording to the cone at the next point, roughly 2⅛" from the original point, below the red trim. Continue in this manner until you reach the back seam; do not cut the cording. Leave more slack in the cording, roughly ¼" lower than the first drape. Glue the cording at the same points as the first row, but below the original cording. At the back seam add more slack to the cording, dropping the swags ½" below the previous row. Continue around the cone in the same manner as before, securing with glue in the same manner. Trim the end at the back seam. Apply one ribbon rose over each point of gathered cording using a glue gun. To finish the inside, measure and cut two 13" lengths of red cording and one 13" length of red grosgrain ribbon. Glue one cording length to the inside top lip of the cone. Below that, glue the length of grosgrain ribbon. Below that, glue the final length of red cording. To apply the green grosgrain ribbon handle, follow the directions for the solid green favor cup.

Green checked favor cup: Measure and cut 13" lengths of looped fringe, moss green cording, and braided trim. Glue the cotton header of the looped fringe to the inside lip of the cone. Glue the length of cording on the outside, right below the looped fringe. Glue the red braided trim below the cording. Glue on the ribbon roses in three rows around the cone as shown in the photo. Space the roses about 2" apart in the top row, about 1¾" apart in the middle row, and about 1⅝" apart in the bottom row. Space the rows about 1½" apart. To finish the inside, measure and cut two 13" lengths of green cording and one 13" length of red grosgrain ribbon. Glue one length of cording to the inside top lip. Below that, glue the length of ribbon, and below that glue the second length of cording. To apply the red grosgrain handle, follow the directions for the solid green favor cup.

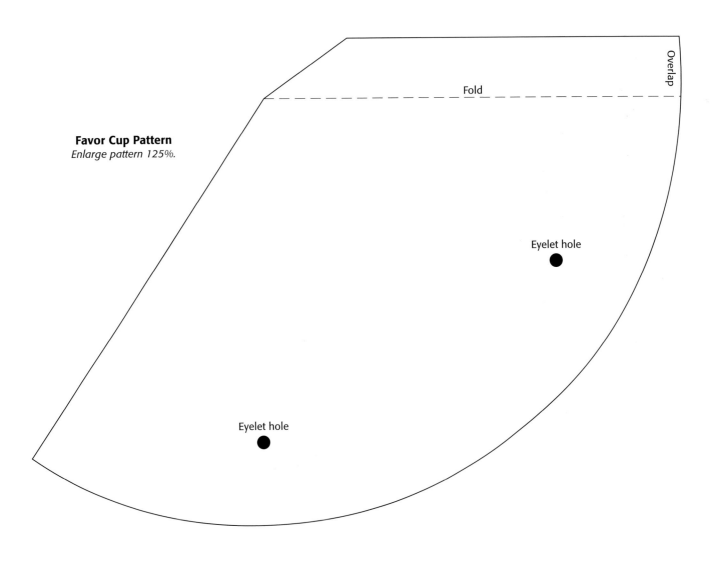

Favor Cup Pattern
Enlarge pattern 125%.

Fold

Overlap

Eyelet hole

Eyelet hole

STENCILED CHRISTMAS WELCOME MAT

BY GENEVIEVE A. STERBENZ

Simple stenciling is all that is required to create this festive welcome mat for the holidays. Begin the design by stenciling the tree in the center. The tree then becomes the backdrop for the cheerful holiday message scribed in red. The big dots in white add another layer to the design, as if snowflakes have left a snowy dusting on the letters themselves.

Materials

+ 2' x 3' jute rug, undyed, with green fabric border
+ Fabric paint in green, brown, red, and white
+ Access to a photocopy machine
+ 6" uppercase letter stencils in brush type (Perfect Letters by the C-Thru Ruler Co.)
+ 6" lowercase letter stencils in brush type (Perfect Letters by the C-Thru Ruler Co.)
+ 14" square of corrugated cardboard
+ 6" square of corrugated cardboard
+ Newspaper
+ Masking tape
+ Spray adhesive
+ Clear acrylic aerosol sealer in matte finish
+ New pencil with eraser
+ Mat knife
+ Self-healing cutting mat
+ Stencil brushes
+ X-Acto knife
+ Small flat paintbrush

DESIGNER'S TIPS

+ To ensure clean lines when stenciling, always apply paint in a pouncing motion from directly above. Don't sweep the paint back and forth.

+ For the letters that are applied over the painted green tree, you may have to apply two coats of paint to get adequate coverage.

+ Caution: Always use aerosol matte sealer in a properly ventilated area.

Instructions

1. Photocopy the patterns on page 95 onto paper. Place the rug right side up on a clean work surface. On a second work surface, place a self-healing cutting mat. Position a 14" square of cardboard on the mat. Cover a third work surface with newspaper. Place the tree pattern wrong side up on the newspaper. Apply a light coat of spray adhesive. Turn the pattern over to the right side and center it on the cardboard. Smooth the pattern flat with your hands. Position the 6" square of cardboard on a work surface and place the snowflake pattern, wrong side up, on clean newspaper. Apply a light coat of spray adhesive. Turn the pattern to the right side and position it on the center of the cardboard. Smooth it flat.

2. For the tree stencil, refer to the cutting diagram below and cut it out around the A line only, using a mat knife to cut straighter lines and an X-Acto knife to cut the curvier lines. Remove the center tree piece and set it aside. Take the 14" piece of cardboard and center it on the rug. Secure it in place with masking tape. Place the snowflake stencil on the self-healing mat and cut along the marked line using an X-Acto knife. Discard the center circle and set the stencil aside.

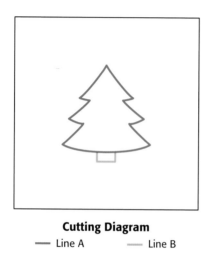

Cutting Diagram
— Line A   — Line B

3. Apply green paint to the exposed rug area in the center of the tree stencil, using a stencil brush. Remove the masking tape and lift off the pattern. Return the pattern to the self-healing mat and cut around line B. When the painted tree has dried, place a strip of masking tape on the rug along the bottom of the tree, above the trunk, and position the pattern on the rug once again. Apply brown paint to the trunk area of the stencil, using a stencil brush. When dry, remove the cardboard stencil and masking tape.

4. Cut out all appropriate letters to spell "Merry Christmas" from stencil sheets using scissors. Then place the letters on the rug to spell the greeting. Since the letter cutouts are the exact size that the stencils will be, you can accurately figure out their placement and spacing.

When you have decided on letter placement, tape down the letters using masking tape. Use a straightedge and the weave of the jute to ensure that all the letters are on the same horizontal plane. Begin with the *M* in *Merry*. Place the stencil over the letter cutout that is taped to the rug so that the cutout fits within the window of the stencil perfectly. Once the stencil is in place, use masking tape to secure one side. Lift the stencil up gently, remove the cutout, and lay the stencil back down. Tape the remaining three sides. Apply red paint using a stencil brush. Lift off the stencil and let the paint dry. Repeat these steps for the remaining letters. To create the highlights on the letters, use a paintbrush to apply white paint along the left and top edges of the letters, as shown in the photograph and the color plan on page 95.

5. Position the circle snowflake stencil on the rug using the color plan on page 95 as a guide. Use masking tape to secure the edges. Apply white paint using a stencil brush. Lift off the stencil and let the paint dry. Repeat around the rug until the desired effect is achieved.

6. Run masking tape along both edges of the inner border to ensure clean edges, and then paint the border red. If your rug doesn't have an inner border, you can create one by running masking tape along the inner edge of the outer border and then again ½" away. Then paint the exposed area red. Let the paint dry and remove the tape. To create outside dots, dip the eraser end of a new pencil in white paint and press onto the green fabric border as you would a rubber stamp. Reapply paint every few dots, going around the entire outside border and spacing dots about ¼" apart.

7. Tape off the outside fabric border of your rug using masking tape. Apply a light coat of clear acrylic sealer to the rug. Let it dry.